The DIAAY (Do It Almost All Yourself) Utility Patenting Classic

Utility Patenting
for IP SAVVYS

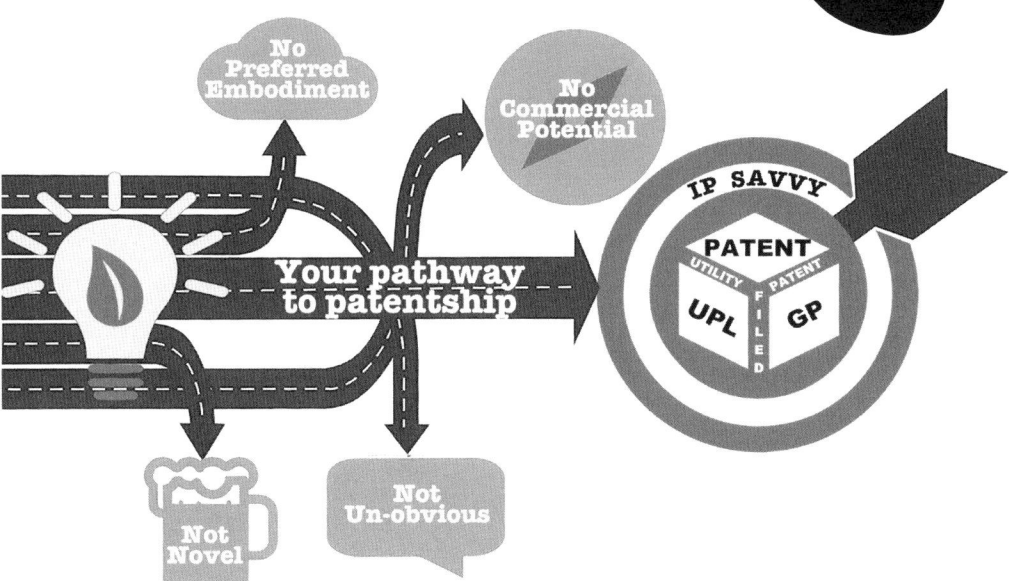

David Schwartz

ISBN: 978-1-09839-156-0
eBook ISBN: 978-1-09839-157-7

Table of Contents

How to read this book and how it is organized

This book is streamlined to be read in one sitting. *IP Savvy* is for both innovator and patent counsel. In a fast look at a very complex domain, I confirm both what you know and what you don't know. I offer a serial inventor/entrepreneur point of view on utility patenting. *IP Savvy* is based on trade secrets from my own thirty-year *pro se* dash down the utility patenting corridor of uncertainty. As a *pro se* global patent holder, I licensed and received substantial royalties on sales of my patented products. I have captured the lessons learned here, as well as in my online course, "Intellectual Property BoostCamp" (IP-BC). My purpose is to demystify how to get utility patents with sustainable competitive advantage (SCA). My perspective is different from the views, guidance, and opinions you will receive from other cohorts in your IP hunt. What you find here is a discussion of critical events and conversation points that occur along the utility patenting pathway and ways to change them.

Choosing how you walk down the IP corridor of uncertainty is a self-management process using the guidance I provide. As in any complex field, there are truths and myths. This book is my best effort to dispel untruths as well as to educate you on some of the trade-offs that are unavoidably part of the corridor's reality. This story is shared in two parts.

In Part 1 I have placed many *Manual of Patent Examination Procedure* (MPEP) rules. Here I make an effort to share utility patent basics, in compliance with the legal framework of the MPEP. I treat the fundamentals of what a utility patent is and the predetermined sequence of steps you will take to get one. I make a singular effort to lay out the rules and not to interpret or posture them. I do this without using legalese or burdening the discussion with alarmist concerns, seeking to present the facts and nothing but the facts.

Part 2 is about changing the utility patenting conversation. I uncover the more subjective dimensions of utility patenting. I do this in two ways. I use the section on drafting to get everyone on the same page with my universal patenting language (UPL) and my set of guiding principles (GP). The UPL ensures everyone is using the same language to describe what's needed to get airtight utility patents, filed first, with real SCA. The guiding principles are my way to handle the patenting process, including a set of utility patent drafting principles that I call the Schwartz Method. Guiding principle semantics also incorporate my big bang theory (BBT) of IP capitalization, explaining patent tactics and how to incorporate utility patenting into the product development life cycle. Further, I offer my conversation-changing guidance by directly rebutting some of the utility patenting myths, identifying trade-offs you have when making choices down the pathway to patentship.

MPEP is the legal framework that provides the true universal patenting language and guiding principles for securing a utility patent. In this book, I offer my UPL and GP as a set of non-legalese terms to allow anyone to be compliant in capturing an invention and converting it to a patent application. My universal patenting language and guiding principles convey complete MPEP compliance and make the construction of a patent readily understood and executed. You will find the basic grammar and semantics for UPL and GP in the glossary. I recommend taking a close look over the glossary before digging into Part 1 and Part 2 of IP SAVVYS. Do this once, before beginning. Then, when you are ready to read Part2, review the glossary one more time in order to increase your understanding and retention of the utility patenting, conversation changing positions that I offer in Part 2.

Your takeaways: The innovator will gain critical insight on how to self-manage their IP journey. For them, this is not a do-it-yourself proposition, but guidelines for what I call a "do it almost all yourself" (DIAAY) approach. It serves as the foundation for changing the conversation about utility patenting with IP counsel. Patent counsel will see all of this differently. They will see a new way to improve their clients' organization with critical insights into patenting language and guidelines. For those who will, this can also offer new ways to help their clients be IP savvy—that is, walk their talk. Patent counsel can encourage their clients to learn Schwartz's UPL and GP as well as to use the IP-BC course levels to achieve higher-quality utility patents faster, while doing so with sensible IP spends, mutual trust, clear and concise dialogue, and aligned work product.

The MPEP rules shared in Part 1 represent my best effort to present the procedures accurately and in readily consumable form. The opinions shared in Part 2 are solely mine and are not legal advice. They are based on my personal experience, and I rest on them. In other words, I sleep well because I knew them to be my truths as I navigated down my IP corridor of uncertainty. They worked for me. I'm sharing them here because I believe some or all of them can work for you. If you do the hard work, you will be rewarded with a notice of allowance (NOA) on a utility patent for your invention, comprised of a supporting specification and claims scoped to the monopoly rights you sought when you started your journey, all at a reasonable cost you can justify.

This book is written with the intention of being both a stand-alone resource as well as a stand-among guide. The stand-alone view seeks to offer a complete roadmap of the rules and steps to get a published utility patent. It reveals the fundamentals and is designed to help you confirm what you know as well as identify what you are less sure about or really don't know. The stand-among view seeks to couple IP SAVVYS, especially Part 2, with my on-line course IP-BC. It reveals the ins and outs of how to construct an airtight patent, offering the basics of using the Schwartz method (TSM) for patent drafting. To augment using TSM, the IP-BC course is provided in levels targeted to your utility patenting role and tasking. Use the coupon to take the course IP-BC/ADVANCED and augment your insight with step by step how to details on deploying TSM.

About your author:
David Charles Schwartz

Dave Schwartz began building his patent portfolio in 1989 as founder and CEO of Productive Environments, LLC. He filed *pro se*, prosecuted to publishing, and licensed his global patents over a twenty-year journey down the IP corridor of uncertainty.

Fig. 1 David Charles Schwartz, IP SAVVYS author and IP-BC course creator

Today Dave's mission, as VP Intellectual Property ESERVGO, is to get you IP savvy. Dave is not an attorney. His value proposition is that he authored his IP-BC course and this book from a serial inventor/entrepreneur's point of view. He delivers a complete MPEP-compliant utility patenting self-management system as a DIAAY framework for preparing and filing airtight utility patents at the lowest practical legal cost.

Dave has distilled his years of IP experience into a readily consumed utility patenting framework with *IP Savvy* and IP-BC. This book is designed to work with the course. The contents benefit from Dave's progressive patenting experience in mechanical objects, computer architecture, artificial intelligence, software-engineered products, robotics, medical devices, electronic devices, FDA pharmaceutical GDP processes, and educational products. He is recognized as an expert in IP creation, acquisition, strategy, and licensing; product/industry marketing; and complex business-to-business selling. Dave is credited with founding, managing, and growing three start-up companies. He has his BSEE from Cornell University, where he was the McMullen Scholar. His MSEE is from MIT and his MBA is from Boston University School of Management.

Dave continues his innovative work in the field of medical devices, where he is developing new personal medical technologies. This is Dave's second book. He is recognized for inventing and patenting the first surface computer and using his innovation for improving organizing literacy in his book *A Crash Course on the Intelligence of Organizing*.

As an engineer by original training, he was a bit of an anomaly in that he reveled in the English language and loved to write. He excelled in his English classes, learned multiple languages, and worked on expanding his personal vocabulary at every opportunity. That said, he is not a literary author who has achieved a compelling writing style that captures imaginations out of the box. Nonetheless, in this book, he persists with the goal of communicating his deep utility patenting experience and understanding in simple language with meaning all can understand and benefit from. To the degree he has achieved this with his IP SAVVYS book and IP-BC course, you will be the judge and jury. Read this book and take the course in the spirit it is offered, and you will reap the rewards from his critical insights and utility patenting guidelines.

Prologue: The Schwartz Method

IP Savvy seeks to offer both innovator and patent counsel a mutual way to get their arms around the complex domain of utility patenting. The way that all IP hunters can do this is to get into the IP Zone, where they can share, agree on, and use my UPL and GP for constructive utility patenting. Part 1 explains the MPEP framework in simple language. Part 2 addresses changing the utility patenting conversation, and as I explained, you can increase your benefits by using the complementary course material in IP-BC. When you really want to change your IP conversation, use the coupon provided, take IP-BC/ADVANCED, and help yourself and your cohorts navigate directly into the IP Zone.

Why put my book into the mix? As an innovator, I wanted to offer a functional approach to utility patenting from an inventor/innovator/entrepreneur point of view that will enable innovators and patent counsel alike to improve their workflow, change their conversations about getting and keeping utility patents, and work more effectively as a team. The MPEP objectively and precisely defines what a utility patent is. It is a legal, rule-based patent framework. When you open it and read it, even though it has everything you need to know, it will prove to be overwhelming. Many books cover the MPEP. Some, like *Patent it Yourself* (Pressman), are extremely helpful, while others all too often intertwine MPEP details with subjective interpretation that borders on fear tactics. This can confuse more than help, as well as result in misunderstanding, trepidation, and consternation.

One of the most important insights I hope to share is how innovators who do more of the utility patenting tasks firsthand benefit the most. They benefit before, during, and after the patent gambit. My GP framework is tied in with the delivery of my UPL, a singular way to talk about patent structure and construction. There's an example of a guiding principle from the field of graphical user interface design in computer software: what you see is what you get (WYSIWYG) (pronounced wizzywig). My expression for utility patenting is what you see is not how you get (WYSINHYG) (pronounced wizznhig). This insight is one of the guiding principles (angles) I use in this book and in my online course, especially the IP-BC/ADVANCED-PRAC-TITIONER level on how to get an airtight utility patent.

Fig.2 A formal utility patent – the Holy Grail

One of my first guiding principles relates to how you look at the formal structure of a utility patent, what I refer to as the Holy Grail. The formal structure is well known—specifically how it is published, section by section. In the Schwartz Method, I share what I call the Schwartz Patent Rubric using my innovator point of view in what I hope will be a more useful way to get the upper hand on the complexity and critical aspects of the utility patenting conversation. This principle unpacks how you build a utility patent from the inside out.

The reason for putting Part 1 first is to define the structure of a patent in a way everyone can agree on. In Part 2, I use WYSINHYG, the Schwartz Method, and the big bang theory to show how to reverse engineer that structure, offering a way to incrementally build a patent as you develop your product. With a repeatable, iterative sequence of steps, you can apply my patent engineering discipline to automatically construct a utility-compliant non-provisional patent at the same time your product pops out. In Part 1, I consistently use MPEP rules as guideposts to present the fundamental patent construct, including a basic definition of drafting. By contrast, in the Part 2 section on drafting, I share insight into how to use my UPL and GP framework to create an airtight utility patent that is right the first time. There, I offer a more in-depth look into the Schwartz Method and how it works. In Part 1, I share the facts and nothing but the facts, including a look at two critical dimensions of utility patents: (1) patent eligibility and (2) patent novelty and nonobviousness. I cover the basic facts about the two dimensions of patentability and how they relate to prior art. By contrast, in Part 2, I cover this topic again in both the section on drafting and in sections on patent tactics and strategies, where the discussion takes a more subjective look into best practices.

PART 1 Basics of what the utility patenting conversation is all about

1.0   Patent construct fundamentals

1.1 Patent basics: What is a patent?

A patent is an asset that has an owner, typically the author. It was most likely created by you as author and your patent counsel. It was examined and granted by your patent office. It conveys what is known as an IP right—a legal right derived from the US Constitution. As we develop all of these points about utility patents, keep in mind the simple idea of the players: the patent office is the publisher, the author (probably you), and the editor (probably your patent counsel).

Patents are granted to an inventor and assigned to an owner, which ultimately may or may not be the inventor (see ownership considerations in the following section). The right conveyed is known as a monopoly right, allowing the owner to exclude others from making, using, offering for sale, or selling the invention throughout the United States, as well as preventing others from importing the invention into the United States. Patents have a life that is a predetermined time period defined as seventeen years from the date of issuance, or twenty years from the date of filing, whichever is shorter. In exchange, the patent application that is filed must make a complete disclosure of the object of the invention for the thing you seek to protect.

1.2 The patent structure

Regarding the legal structure, to be compliant with the MPEP, a patent is used to claim an invention in a legal document that includes the following sections:

Title—A short label for the invention. It can be descriptive. Many times, a succinct simplification of the first claim in the invention is used. I will keep to the definitions here and save insights for the follow-up section on drafting.

Field of the invention—Defines the area of technology using terms from the predefined classification of subject matter for the object of the invention.

Background—Describes the current state of the application art conveying the "world" in which the invention will interoperate. It shares the limitations of the existing objects of invention and forms the case in which your invention's claimed scope will be allowable.

Summary—The summary is formed as a simplified statement of each of the claims, nothing more and nothing less. It is a literal summary of the claims.

Brief description of the drawings/figures—A set of figures with a short, one-sentence summary of what each one is.

Figures/drawings—In advance of the detailed description, they follow the numbers used in the brief description and provide visual details of all of the structural elements in your invention and how they fit together. Each figure's parts are uniquely identified with reference numbers.

Detailed description—Contains a full explanation of the invention in sufficient detail for anyone skilled in the art to make and use your invention, including all the details of what it is and how it works. It is here that the reference numbers for the elements of the invention shown in the figures must be definitely used, consistently using the same names (terms) and the same reference numbers to describe each element and how they work together to create the unexpected behavior.

Claims—The claims section is the last part of the patent application. It begins with the number 1 and increments by one for each claim that follows. Each claim is a run-on sentence that identifies each part of the invention and how it is put together. It must be on eligible subject matter, and it must be novel and unobvious with respect to the prior art. It is the basis on which you seek your monopoly rights, explicitly scoping the aspects of the preferred embodiment (P-E) you seek to prevent others from making, using, or selling.

Abstract—The abstract of the invention is always the last page but is published as the first page if your application is allowed. It is a summary of the core aspects of the invention using 150 words or less. Think of it as a marketing tweet to the examiner, letting him or her know that you know what your invention really is.

1.3 What is patentable and what is required for a compliant patent application

The object of the invention constructed in the patent application must be both eligible for patenting and unique in its definition (specification). It must be described in sufficient detail to enable one skilled in the art to practice it (i.e., implement the invention) without a lot of fooling around. This filed document must represent the invention in its P-E, which is the best mode for practicing the invention known to the inventor at that time.

A variety of inventions are protectable by a patent. Typically, objects of invention include gadgets, medical devices, tools, methods for making or using things, computer software, pharmaceuticals, and materials made by man that are not naturally occurring. At the end of the day, each of these may earn protected rights so long as they are represented with sufficient "enablement" in their field of art (*field of art* is a term derived from the classification within which the right is sought) and the threshold for enablement is nuanced in each classification, with software and pharmaceuticals among the more challenging.

Further, the representation of the P-E of the invention can and must be in at least one of the following: in the form of a process or method, a machine, an item of manufacture, or a composition of matter. A process is generally a sequence of steps. A machine is generally a real thing, often comprising a combination of parts that perform a function, solve a problem, and produce a result. Items of manufacture are articles produced from raw or processed materials yielding new forms or combinations with new qualities and/or properties, whether produced by hand labor or by a machine. Compositions of matter involve creations from two or more substances.

They can be formed from any composite article, made with a chemical union and/or a mixture, or formed as gases, fluids, powders, or solids.

Enablement is the definite and unambiguous explanation of how the invention works. For now, you can expect that if your idea is eligible, and if it is truly novel, when you do the hard work to get it on file, it will result in a utility patent with reasonably claimed scope.

What's the hard work? Your patent requires a clear description that is both definite in structure and function (not ambiguous), and that discloses some form of delightfully unanticipated but discoverable behavior that has a practical use, often referred to as utility. It must include at least one claim that explicitly and unambiguously articulates the innovation—that is, the claim must "read on" the specific P-E using terms that are definite and consistently used throughout the patent. The monopoly right, if granted, covers only the claim in an allowed, issued, and published patent. Patents are granted after being examined on their merits during what is called prosecution. During prosecution, the patent is investigated by an examiner and a determination is made as to whether the claim(s) are allowable. If a notice of allowance is granted, the patent is given a publishing date. If you file internationally, you will have multiple prosecutions to manage. Since the monopoly right is constrained solely by its supported, definite claim(s), it does not turn on anything else. In other words, anything said about it in the patent specification's body matters only insofar as it supports the claim(s). At the end of the day, that's the long and the short of it.

Converting an idea into a filed and subsequently published patent is tied to the state it is in along the pathway to patentship. In the process, once the invention is converted into a legal patent document and filed, it is either a "pending application" or an "issued patent." It's kind of obvious, but it's an important distinction, insofar as calling something a utility patent without saying utility patent application means it's an issued right. When a patent is pending, it means it's been filed but not (fully) examined on its merits (i.e., it hasn't been prosecuted at the US Patent Office and allowed to issue).

1.4 Patentability: Eligibility, novelty, nonobviousness

When all is said and done, a lot more is said than done. I am all about not writing bible patents (the greatest story ever told) with weak or unsupported claims. The essence of what you get turns on patentability.

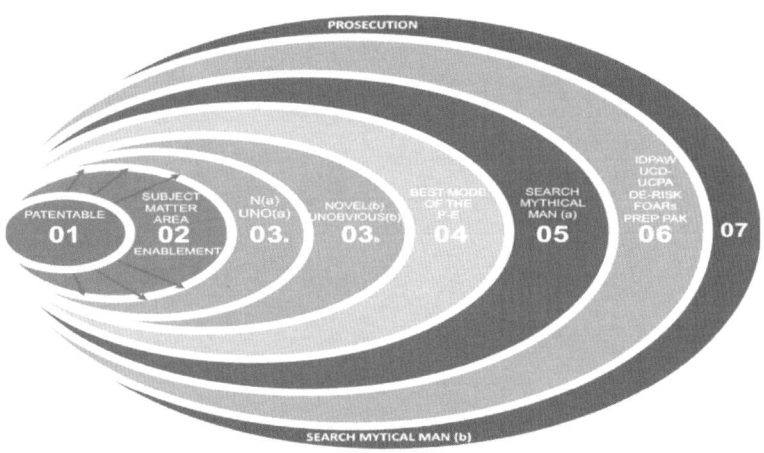

Fig.3 The onion peel view of patentability

One way to think about this is to envision an onion peel. When an examiner is assessing whether the object of your invention is patentable, their first consideration is patent-eligible subject matter. After this, novelty or uniqueness must be investigated and established.

Then nonobviousness is sorted out. Novelty and nonobviousness are delicately intertwined.

You will see that you can emulate the examiner before you file by applying UPL/GP to your utility patenting workflow. It is important to separate out the application of the rules for patentability for the interval before filing and after allowance. For this brief discussion, I'm pointing at the examiner's use before allowing, even though the foundational aspects of using the rules are identical.

Eligible P-Es include any new and useful process, machine, manufacture, composition of matter, or any new and useful improvement thereof. Uniqueness is referred to as novelty. The invention must be new and different from the prior art that came before it. Keeping this onion peel in mind, the notion of examination for obviousness has its proper place in the process. In order to not be ruled on as being obvious, it must be "nonobvious," meaning that the difference between the invention and the prior art must create what is often referred to as an ah-ha moment to anyone else of ordinary skill in the art looking at the invention. This is arguably a subjective turning point, but that's the deal. At the European Patent Office (EPO), examination for nonobviousness is also referred to as finding, showing, and having an "inventive step" over the prior art. Since the harmonization of European and US patent laws, the ideas are basically equivalent.

As you would expect, patent laws exclude some things from being patented. Humans are not patentable. Contracts between two parties do not fit the bill. Perpetual motion machines are not allowed. Natural substances—that is, substances found in nature—are not eligible. Algorithms representing abstract ideas can be rejected while software implemented on hardware that results in a practical application, typically depicted as a transformation of data, may be patentable.

1.5 Ownership considerations

In simple terms, you own your patent unless or until, for any one of a number of reasons, you cause its loss—and then you don't. When an invention is created by an inventor or inventors, and a patent application is drafted and filed with a claim that incorporates specific parts he or she contributed to, then they are listed on the patent, with the lead inventor the one who holds sway on the construct known as the first independent claim. The question of ownership remains open. The fact that the inventors are named does not convey ownership rights. Ownership rights may be transferred at any time but are unequivocally assigned at the time of filing. Typically, a lone wolf inventor (rarer these days) will assign the application to themselves at filing and thereby establish a chain of ownership where they own 100 percent of the patent rights on issue. If an inventor is an employee, when they were hired, nine times out of ten, they signed a confidentiality and assignment agreement in which they ceded the rights to any invention made while employed to their employer. In that scenario, a company will usually create a bill of sale for each inventor on the subsequent development of a patentable idea, where the right for that instance of the invention is turned over to the company for a sum of one dollar. Of course, use cases can become more complicated.

Each inventor with a contribution in a filed claim will provide their name, physical residential address, and country of citizenship. The inventors must be legitimate with respect to the contribution and the part of the claim attributed to them. Further, if you leave off someone who should have been listed, that can make the patent unenforceable if they successfully press their right at a later time. When there is a plurality of inventors, any inventors who have not assigned their rights in some way each own 100 percent of the patent. This means that in absence of any prior assignment, the joint owners as individuals may make, use, offer to sell, or sell the patented invention within the United States, or prevent the import of the patented invention into the United States, without the consent of and without reporting to any others. If for any reason, you are under any obligation to assign any rights in the invention to others not in the company, that's a crucial element and it will need to be taken into consideration in order to establish the best way to have the ownership of the patent application or eventual patent properly identified and assigned.

1.6 The formal process of converting an idea to a patent

Issued patents are formal legal documents. In discussing the patent document in this section, I want to restate I am not covering the Schwartz Method and Schwartz patent rubric here. As you will find out, the method of creating a patent is an engineering discipline and the universal language and guidance on how to do it are explained in the Schwartz Method.

One of your first considerations will be whether or not you have a patentable invention. This is a complex consideration and turns on a variety of considerations not limited to your ability to articulate the true preferred-embodiment (P-E) of your inventive concept, whether it has novelty (read that uniqueness), and whether or not it existed before in a like or similar embodiment with utility in any field of use. Rather than try to sort out those issues now, I will cover them in detail throughout Part 1 and in the beginning of Part 2. For now, the point is to explain what the conversion process is under the assumption that you have decided to patent the object of your invention.

It's straightforward to explain what a patent looks like when it's MPEP compliant. This is a fundamentally different train of thought from the best way to represent the preferred object of your invention in such a form that it can be converted into a patent application. When we get to the drafting step, you will see how what you see is not how you get it. When you have a foundation with insider understanding of what makes a great patent—that is, a patent rubric—you will understand the inside-out nature of what a patent must embody in order to be an airtight representation of your invention. I convey all of this later on without using legal mumbo jumbo "patentease." Know this critical information and you will be able to complete your own audit as if you were the examiner before filing, so you get it right the first time.

It's almost unnervingly straightforward to detail the MPEP framework for what a patent must look like on filing it. The purpose of this book and of my online course is to show a pathway to drafting and publishing. As with any complex idea, a metaphor can be a gift to aid understanding.

In explaining this, I use a metaphor by comparing the process of patenting to publishing a great novel. You write your epic novel, turning your invention story into a protected object of invention (i.e., a utility patent) and do so in the most compelling, most accurate, least complex, least expensive, and fastest way possible. The best way to write and publish your non-provisional patent (your "novel") is to use my UPL and guiding principles as you separate out the essence of your idea and turn it into a patentable intermediate form that is MPEP compliant. Patent drafting principles are the foundation stones you will tread on the pathway to patentship.

2.0 Getting the patent: From trade secret to drafting, filing, prosecution, and allowance

---

2.1 Your idea is a trade secret until it isn't: Trade secrets

Now that you know what a patent (application) looks like along with the sequence of events from ideation and invention capture through the stages of publishing, let's focus on the development of a utility-compliant patent application as a trade secret and the form of patent you convert it to.

Trade secrets are not registered or filed. Instead, they are maintained by their owners using protocols that mark trade secrets as confidential and secret, where limits are put on access. Trade secret protection ends once the secret is publicly disclosed.

When you first molded your idea into a concrete form, you probably began thinking about constructing a patent application for it. You were entertaining the legal goal of getting a monopoly right for the claims in that patent if and when it published.

Fig 4. The Flash Of Genius – coming out of the FOG

Here I liken the process of invention to a flash of genius (FOG). Think of it as coming out of the FOG as you perfect your P-E for the object of your invention. More on this in my blog on FOG (https://www.ipboostcamp as a member you can access my complete blog). In every situation, when the idea is nascent and in an early form of representation, it is a trade secret. No one knows about it except for you and your cohorts.

Typically, when people talk about trade secrets, they have a more general definition. The description includes tangible and/or intangible information. Critically, the owner of that information seeks to prevent competitors (or the public) from learning about it in order to enjoy a competitive advantage in the marketplace. In order to keep it (think the formula for colored glass), the information must be treated in a way that can reasonably be expected to keep it private, except in cases of improper acquisition or theft.

A lot of trade secrets revolve around things like customer lists, workflow methods, social marketing parameters etc. Here I focus solely on your invention. Some of your secrets may pass through both your business filter and patentability filters, emerging as targets for patenting. Not all secrets warrant patents. Look at your formulas and algorithms (including computer algorithms), patterns, devices, ideas, processes, lists, recipes, strategies, internal systems for processing information, business or advertising strategies, and manufacturing techniques. If they cannot be readily figured out (reverse engineered) by anyone deconstructing the end product or outcome, they can remain secrets. It doesn't necessarily mean, however, that they are targets for patenting.

The date of the first instance of your invention is referred to as the date of conception. It is important, even in proceedings after the Leahy-Smith America Invents Act (AIA) tied to post-issuance petitions, ownership, and royalties. As promised, I will defer the tactics and strategies for patents until after the fundamental concepts are developed, so more on that later. For now, understand that your patentable idea is a secret unless or until you act in a way that makes it public domain.

To be clear, compared to the date of conception, the filing date of your invention is the date when you hit the patent office whether with either a provisional (reference the one-year rule, discussed later) or a non-provisional patent application. The AIA makes the United States a first-to-file country. Even though the United States is no longer a first-to-invent country, I will cover some cases in *ex parte* proceedings where it may be helpful to have a proven and document-ed date of conception. Since it is often difficult to reconstruct this date as time passes, when you use Schwartz's *Invention Disclosure Patent Application Workbook* (IDPAW) diligently, you will always have both the conception date as well as the filing date on record. Be sure to get confirmation of the IDPAW P-E version entries by a cohort when you are archive each iteration as taught in IP-BC's the

Schwartz Method. All references to the IP-BC course can be followed at the course website https://www.ipboostcamp.com .

Now, let's put this in the context of patentable matter. Your invention (as opposed to a customer list or a process formulation for colored glass), from the date of its conception up until a patent on it is published, is a (trade) secret if you take the proper care and precautions not to disclose it publicly. Even after filing, if you decide not to file internationally, and indicate so in your filing packet, your application will not be published until it is allowed. If you don't so indicate, then it will qualify for filing globally, and whether you ultimately do or don't, after eighteen months it will automatically be published, along with all the claims in your specification (re: harmonization with global patent practices). Otherwise, it will remain a trade secret unless and until it is allowed and published. Keep in mind that since the United States is a first-to-file (instead of a first-to-invent) country, if a third party independently invents your idea using their own inventive process, and they file a patent on it before you (i.e., first), and successfully prosecute it to completion, they can get the monopoly rights for that idea, even though you might have conceived of it first.

2.2 Drafting basics

Drafting is the way you constructively turn your invention description into a legal document that can be examined on its merits for the award of a utility patent. It is a slippery slope since there can be many stages in converting your idea into a formal non-provisional utility patent application.

For this reason, I separate out the heavy lifting of the "engineering science" of drafting into Part 2. In Part 1, I include a discussion about drafting as a step in the sequence of events so the entire conversion process can be explored and understood. In Part 2, I explain why drafting is not an abstract art to be practiced only by IP shamans. There I detail what drafting is really all about and how to use the Schwartz Method to get an SCA patent application into play.

This book and my course hold a single purpose in using the Schwartz Method: to integrate the development of the patent application into the product development life cycle. As such, there are steps along the way when your invention will appear more and more like a patentable object, and each version of the story you tell about it approaches the best, right-first-time patent application you can file conterminously with the release of the product embodied by the claims in that patent application.

When we work through the fundamentals of what a patent is, a simple idea will help us separate the invention and its merits from the patent document itself and its merits. If you were the creator of a new story you wanted to publish in a book, you would craft your creative vision into a readable form that you would seek to have edited and published. If your story was truly original and a publisher agreed to turn it into a readable book and market it, then readership would determine if you made it to the *NY Times* bestseller list. If you copied the idea from someone, you would be stopped at the pass or found guilty of fraud after the fact.

Explaining patent construction benefits from a return to the metaphor of publishing an epic novel. Your idea might or might not make it to the *NY Times* bestseller list—in our case, making it through the corridor of patenting uncertainty to be published as an allowed patent. Its successful transition will be determined by its originality as well as its business model and commercial value. I make a concerted effort to distinguish between the draft of your object of invention as a utility patent application (i.e., this section) and the crafting of the formal patent application from the draft on your object of invention (later sections, esp. "Drafting guidelines"). The pathway for turning your idea into a patent must turn on the continual refocusing and iteration of your idea into a P-E worthy of patenting, keeping the fuzzy line between the two crisply separated. This separation will allow us insight and better choices of which doors to open down the corridor, with whom, and when.

2.3 Preparation of the DOC PAK and filing in your home country

There are state changes in converting your idea to a patent. The state will change from provisional to non-provisional if you start with a provisional first. In either case, you convert your invention into a patent by getting a patent application drafted (the complete section on drafting is in Part 2). Then a document packet (DOC PAK) is prepared, and it is filed. Once you convert to a non-provisional the pending patent application must be prosecuted to issue. In summary, on filing your application is in one of two states. It is either a provisional patent application or a non-provisional patent application. Each uses a different combination of documents required for filing.

You will find that for each filing choice for your patent application there is a different DOC PAK. That's the term I use for the set of documents required for setting up your patent application and getting it filed. I do not cover the details of what's in a completed DOC PAK here. I do provide a sample with the minimal set of forms for a provisional in IP-BC. Getting a DOC PAK prepared and ready for filing is simple and straightforward.

Patent attorneys as well as patent agents will typically use their paralegals or administrative assistants to prepare the documents that must accompany a patent application filing. In all fairness to the sequence of steps in your IP hunt on the pathway to patentship, this is the easiest, and you can make sure all of the records are prepared and sent to counsel, so they just have to review them and not create them. This will save you money, and when you need to review your package before it's filed, it's going to look like something you're familiar with and the error checks you make before actual filing will be easier. If errors are found in these papers, they will be immediately flagged at the patent office, your application will be held, and you will be given an explanation and a short interval to perfect the papers. Don't rack up wasted patent charges from counsel here. With the right preparation, your filing will be recorded, and you will get a recording date (which documents your filing date) in due course with no other rigmarole. Get these papers right the first time—it really is the easiest and most fun part of getting through the first ring of fire.

2.4 Patent choice (what to file): provisional or non-provisional

Of the two available application forms—provisional and non-provisional—the simpler one is a US provisional application. The provisional application is one way applicants seek an early filing date. Provisional applications are not examined and therefore never issue. This type of application requires completion of basic information including the invention title and the names of the inventor(s). The forms are submitted together with a required filing fee and the substantive patent application document. Provisional applications will include the detailed description of the invention and related figures. A provisional application may be filed without claims (more on this later). The filing date you get starts your one-year rule for that filing. I provide a sample of these forms in IP-BC/ADVANCED. All of these forms can be downloaded from the US Patent Office. When you submit, you can send a hard copy using express mail, but today the most practical approach is to open an account and file everything electronically.

You will find that the US non-provisional application has a more complex set of forms that require all the information required for the provisional application, as well as assignee, applicant, claim(s), claim count, additional documents like the chain of ownership, and an optional information disclosure statement (IDS), all with associated fees. Do not be intimidated by these documents. You have all of this information—just fill it in. No strategy is involved in filling out the forms. Strategy is involved in picking your type of filing, however. Non-provisional applications have strict MPEP requirements for the format and content. The non-provisional application, aka the utility patent application, if allowed, will publish and issue as a utility patent. If you filed a non-provisional application without having a provisional application on file, then the filing date is the filing date. If it publishes, that is the date it gets—there is no need for the one-year rule.

Currently a provisional application filing fee is $280, and a non-provisional application filing fee is $1,720. In the end, the actual fees will depend on number of claims, and this is all a straightforward parameter on the first page of the form for the filing packet.

One of the most important timing issues will be related to your game plan for international filing. Again, I cover this in more detail in Part 2. For now, just remember that in nearly every country, there is a requirement to maintain novelty for that patent application before filing there, meaning the international application must be filed in the designated country or countries before any public disclosure is made anywhere.

The one-year rule applies when using the provisional patent application. This means you have one year from the date of filing of a provisional application on your invention to convert it into a non-provisional application. As long as you keep the invention covered by the claims (if any) confidential, you will not breach your right to file in Paris Convention countries with your US Patent Office filing date.

Typically, if you use the Schwartz Method and file your provisional application right the first time, you can flip it from a provisional application into a non-provisional application without adding new information or changing the scope of the claim(s). As you will see, you're always better off to have at least one claim in your provisional application. Anyone who doesn't have a claim probably has not flushed out their P-E, and that is a recipe for disaster. When using a provisional application, if you don't abandon it, the date you flip it to a non-provisional application is when the clock starts for examination on its merits.

During pendency, for either a provisional or a non-provisional application, you have a key right to place the term "patent pending" on the product or service covered in that application. The mark is valid while your application is pending and hasn't expired or been abandoned. Since a provisional patent application does not require that a claim be submitted with it, this gets to be a grey area. Suffice it to say, you want to stay clear of any misrepresentation in using "patent pending." Further, for all filing and prosecution processes, if you lie to the patent office, you risk being cited for fraud with some hefty fines and reprisals. In any system of democracy, there are laws for crimes and punishments, and the field of utility patenting is no different. When you decide to patent, and you have a patent application on file, then it's not only your right but also your obligation to place "patent pending" on it when it's marketed in any way. The reason for this is to ensure others know you are defining your territory, because if they willfully infringe and you successfully stop them, their penalties could be tripled. If they don't know they are stepping on your grounds, then your options for damages will be curtailed. If you don't include a claim in your provisional, you can still say patent pending however I advise doing this with caution so as not to overreach in your offensive maneuver.

2.5 Prosecution choice: Normal, Priority, Accelerated, Patent Prosecution Highway, and Special Petitions

There are a number of formalities for filing, and each will impact how your prosecution proceeds. When it comes to the choice of how to file, you will want to be aware of all of the ways to file. Here I list their basic features. For any of these, the simple objective is to move your patent application forward in the queue so it can be put on the desk of the examiner in your art group for examination on its merits. Here are basic elements of the filing choices and how they affect prosecution. In Part 2, I cover more on the prosecution request tactics and strategies.

Normal Examination (NE)

Pay your fee based on the number of independent and dependent claims in your non-provisional application and get in line. Waiting times can exceed one or two years depending on the art group you filed in.

Accelerated examination (AE)

If you have no more than three independent and twenty total claims during pendency and you pay an additional fee, you can accelerate the examination of your patent application. I mention some fees here. You must go to the US Patent Office website to check the current fees at the time you proceed. For example, the current fee is $140 for a large entity or $70 for a small entity. The request cannot be made with the filing of a request for continued examination (RCE). If you have to file an RCE, the filing of the RCE during accelerated examination (AE) does not terminate your AE status. If your petition is granted, the US Patent Office will advance you out of turn and commence examination. Accelerated examination has the most stringent requirements, and you are going to have to do most if not all of the work the examiner would do, ahead of time and with filing. Basically, you will need to prepare and file a much more robust form of IDS with a pre-examination search document and an AE support document. If the documents are incomplete, you will not be granted the petition. Your patent must be filed using the figure item numbers in the claim, and you must refer to every piece of art element and claim using that art in the IDS with their item numbers. The pre-examination search document must also include the search logic used. The support document must provide a detailed analysis of how your pending claims are distinguished from the closest prior art you identified using the respective item numbers. See Part 2 on filing tactics and strategy to assess and compare this to a prioritized examination (PE).

Prioritized Examination (PE)

For applications with no more than four independent and a total of thirty claims during pendency, the procedure offers expedited review of a patent application. With PE, you will get a final disposition within twelve months of your initial filing date. This procedure does not mandate a pre-examination search or the stringent document requirements. To do this, you must make your request at the time of filing of your initial application, or if and when seeking to continue prosecution after a final rejection, with your RCE. The fees should always be checked in advance. The patent office is going to have to do a lot more work and much faster, so you are going to have to pay for it. For large entities (500 employees or more), the current fee is $4,000. Small entities (500 employees or fewer) get a discounted fee of $2,000. Start-ups typically qualify as small entities unless they are owned by a large entity or have an exclusive license of a patent from a large entity. For the fee, the US Patent Office's goal is to provide the final disposition within twelve months of the date on which the prioritized status was requested compared to two to four years for regular examination. A final disposition may be a notice of allowance, a final rejection, or a notice of abandonment. To keep to the schedule, you will have only three months to respond to any office action, and you cannot ask for an extension of time. If you miss a deadline, you can file an extension, but you will be returned to normal prosecution. If you get to a final rejection and decide to file an RCE to continue prosecution, PE ends, and you are back to normal prosecution.

Patent Prosecution Highway (PPH)

This form of prosecution can be requested if there is an allowed claim in a corresponding foreign application first, and the examiner in the United States has not yet issued a first office action on the merits. The foreign patent office report can be used in the

US Patent Office as the first step in getting a US allowance for that claim. Check the fee.

Special Petitions (SP)

Petitions to make special can also come into play. A petition to make special can be filed to take your application out of turn. This can be done if (1) at least one of the inventors is over age sixty-five, (2) a request is made by the head of a government agency, (3) the patent relates to the environment, (4) the patent relates to the development of energy, or (5) the patent relates to counterterrorism.

2.6 Filing globally: International filing considerations

If filing globally, you are opting for a downstream sequence of events when you will be prosecuting your patent application at the patent offices in the foreign countries in which you have elected to pursue your monopoly rights. When you have executed a non-provisional patent application in your home country, there is a procedure to use the same application in elected countries. The foreign patent applications will be handled in each country, and where required, translation into the language of that country will be part of that process along with the applicable fees. This will all be handled by registered patent agents or patent attorneys in each country. You will want to take advantage of the Paris Convention for filing in target European geographies. You can opt for these any time during the first year in which you filed in your home country. Typically, these elections are made conterminously with the filing of the applications in your home country (here the United States) by filling in the appropriate form selections. Since the United States is a Paris Convention member, US applicants file first in the United States and then within one year they file in the other foreign countries of their choice. Subsequently, there will be what is called the national phase, which will occur within two to three years from when your initial filing was recorded—that is, your priority date. If you're not careful in paring your patent application down to one invention and tightening up your patent to make it the shortest and most expressly scoped it can be, you are going to be in for a very expensive ride abroad.

The prosecution phase in foreign countries requires preparing and submitting any of your traversals to objections, related arguments, and, undesirably, any amendments in response to any foreign office action to the foreign agent either you or your patent counsel is in league with to file the actual foreign reply. It can get complicated very quickly.

A Paris Cooperation Treaty (PCT) application requires much of the same information as a US non-provisional application, including further variations in the filing packet such as which countries you are filing in, all of which are required before filing. It gets the filing date of the non-provisional application in your country of origin. If it publishes in a designated country, its filing date is assigned the one on your US application. The PCT acts as an international framework for filing patent applications with access to at least 148 countries. The examination with the PCT process does not result in the grant of one, single international patent. Its purpose is to simplify the process of filing foreign applications, to defer the expenses associated with applying for patent protection in the foreign countries you select, and to provide an international patentability search report. With a PCT filing, the filing of each non-provisional application at the national stage is deferred for each country you select by about thirty months from your earliest priority date. Just know you will have to translate your patent application into the native language of each country you select unless they use or accept English. If you don't use the Schwartz Method to ensure your application is tight (the shortest application under the circumstances) and you do file globally, be prepared to dig deep for translation costs.

You will need to comply with all of the formal format and structure points for the non-provisional application as well as for the PCT application. Use my sample DOC PAK to understand how this is set up along with my checklist to make sure you've got everything. Remember that the US Patent and Trademark Office forms site is the only source you need for all of the current forms and fees, along with each variation required for each type of filing.

You may be told that attempting to identify the proper forms and complete them correctly for filing is stressful and not recommended. It is actually easier than filing taxes. You will want to garner the expertise of experienced filers when deciding when and how to file, especially if you are filing globally. Remember the need as well to preserve absolute novelty if you seek to avoid becoming your own prior art.

Since the monopoly rights will be extended to a filer in each country where his or her patent is allowed, the choice of where to file should be linked to the geographies where you believe you will have your best potential sales. Just realize that if you pick one country over another, then a competitor can exercise your patent claims in the countries you don't pick, with impunity.

2.7 Prosecution: Domino theory

In this section, I place prosecution in its natural sequence as an integral step in the conversion of an idea into a patent. I reserve the heavy lifting on prosecution for Part 2 as it is integrally tied to the drafting work covered there. I share key insights on how to make the prosecution part of the process as smooth as possible. Here I explain the basic back-and-forth that occurs with patent office rejections in order to expose the risks. In Part 2, I expand on the use of the Schwartz Method for avoiding FOARs before filing.

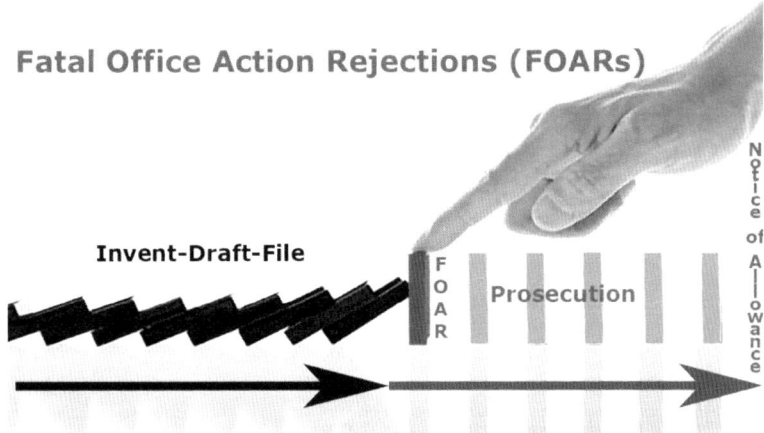

Fig5. Domino sequence, moving from preparation to filing and prosecution

A good way to think about what is happening when moving from preparation to filing and prosecution is to think in terms of a set of dominos in a line. The idea is to tip the first domino over and have the entire sequence of events follow in like falling dominos. If you get stopped with a fatal office action rejection (FOAR), then you will not reach notice of allowance (NOA). The key notion in IP SAVVYS is to make sure you derisk from FOARS before filing. More on this later.

Discussing prosecution will benefit from keeping the before, during, and after time division in mind. The before step is getting the patent application in order, completing all documents, and setting up for payment of all required fees so the application can be filed and recorded. Once recorded, it will be examined in its proper art class in due course. A patent application will sit on the examiner's desk—depending on the rate of queuing in the art unit and the rate of examination of the examiner the art unit is assigned to—for as long as it takes unless you do one of the accelerated filing procedures.

Remember that patent applications in the United States will publish at eighteen months from their earliest priority date unless you don't plan to file globally and request non-publication. Any filed foreign applications will publish in eighteen months. It is entirely possible that your patent application along with all of its claims will publish before prosecution begins, and anyone can have a look at what you've got.

The term *patent prosecution* refers to the sequence of events that occurs after filing a non-provisional patent application that is in condition for examination on its merits. Remember that provisional patent applications sit before prosecution starts. They are not examined, so they never enter the prosecution phase. When a non-provisional patent application is finally examined on its merits, the during phase of patent prosecution has begun. This is a dynamic interval in which the examiner will seek a finding on the allowability of your claims, during which time you will have the right to traverse any of his or her objections in order to secure a properly scoped allowance.

From the time your patent application is filed with the US Patent Office, it can take on order of one year for examination, then one to two years for prosecution (or longer), depending on how it goes, meaning it could be upward of three years before your patent rights are granted.

Unless you abandon your application for some reason, you are locked into prosecuting your patent application once it's filed.

This sequence of events is one of the riskiest parts of the pathway to patentship, in terms of weakening the perceived quality of the application, as well as holding the greatest risks for budget busting. Prosecution will test the mettle of even the savviest IP hunters. Without doubt, this phase is the one planted with the most minefields, and since an issued patent will become a public record, every aspect of your dialogue with the examiner during prosecution will be captured and published in what is called the file wrapper. When that compilation publishes with your issued patent and is discoverable for any purpose by anyone, if you messed up during prosecution, your mistakes will be on show for all to ponder. Rest assured, the Schwartz Method is designed to de-risk your patent application so that if you have an allowable patent claim, it will publish cleanly.

2.8 In the clinches of prosecution with the examiner

Your prosecution will occur within the specific art units of your technology. There are different pending intervals for each art unit, and examiners work at different paces. The job of the examiner during prosecution is to assess patentability. Remember that this includes eligibility as well as novelty and nonobviousness. For eligibility, the examiner applies the current "rules on allowable matter." For novelty and nonobviousness, the examiner performs his or her "mythical person" search in order to establish whether relevant prior art applies.

As a general rule, it is essential to take the iterative exchange with the examiner in the most constructive way possible, even if you get initial rejections on points you consider completely bogus. Try to see the examiner's exchange as a thousand points of light—guidance through the morass of prior art and claim scope. This is the only way you as an applicant are informed by the examiner about the "patent worthiness" of your application. The patent office issues patent office actions, and the applicant responds. This goes on for however long it takes.

At the end of the day, in examination, the examiner will only consider what is claimed in your invention on the date of your filing and compare that to any aspect of the prior art found in order to determine if your stuff is obvious to someone skilled in the art.

Typically, an interview is requested if there is a sticking point, and the applicant believes a direct explanation will facilitate the case. Any inventor is permitted to be the lead in handling this phase, including the right to request and secure a direct interview with the examiner, as well as to petition for a higher review if the examiner finds against the claimed invention and gives a final rejection.

During this process, applicants (as inventors) can represent themselves—if they know what they're doing. If and when an interview is requested, usually the examiner will grant it and give the applicant notice of the time and date. He or she will conduct the discussion with the applicant or an appointed power. The parties end the interview with an agreement on what was discussed and decided, and the examiner confirms by replying with details of the outcome. That paper will also become part of the file wrapper. European Patent Office interview procedures have the same objective (more on this in the section on the points of guidance on alternative ways to handle risk situations during prosecution).

The nature of an examiner's investigation on merit is a little broader. What I mean is that an examiner can throw any aspect of any reference at your patent application. In the case of another patent, the examiner can even use the detailed description to determine your novelty or obviousness, even if the claims in that application cover something else. Basically, the examiner can do anything he or she wants with prior art in order to undermine your claims. The way the examiner does this is to state a determination that the art (or combination) "teaches in the direction" of one or more of your claims.

If eligible, you will receive the first of what I call a fatal office action rejection (FOAR), if and when the examiner is not convinced you are novel and unobvious. You have the right to argue this. This is called traversing the rejection, and you may do this in your reply to that action. This is the examiner's shot across the bow or, worse, the uppercut as a first knockout punch in the slugfest that will ensue. If you haven't done your homework with the Schwartz Method, you may find yourself in a world of hurt. There are a variety of FOARs to consider, and I cover them in Part 2 of the drafting section. The rejections can appear inscrutable unless and until you fully understand what it means to draft an airtight utility patent.

Some of the other rejections based on patent compliance might be combined in a single office action, citing multiple rejections. On the issue of eligibility and nonobviousness, it's worth summarizing. When the question of patentability and obviousness is on the table, you must traverse it first. When rejections are made based on obviousness, they are typically made first and can use either one very compelling piece of prior art, or, at the examiner's discretion, the combination of a plurality of prior art references (prior patents, published applications and uses, etc.) that "teach" your novelty—that is, the essential aspects claimed in your patent application for your invention. In a traversal reply, made within a predetermined time, the responder restates an accurate summary of everything the examiner said in order to reply to each objection separately, line by line, referring to the examiner's points, whether in sequence or in a combination. The objective is to help the examiner see why the rejection(s) was/were baseless. All language must remain positive, and no statement that undermines the filing should be made, either accidently or intentionally.

The formation of a response to an office action follows a very simple format and is very much like a natural dialogue as in any debate. The format is designed to be read by the world, so its single purpose is to establish clarity on what is being separated out, found relevant, and either acceptable or not without any ambiguity for any party to the reading. It is essential to echo the examiner's points in sequence and to respond to each one with a focused traversal.

Typically, in the traversal, the applicant gently shows the examiner the error of their ways by identifying supporting pointers from the applicant's patent specifications (figures, description, identification of the delightful/unexpected behavior, and utility) and showing how the applicant's claimed invention "teaches away" from the cited art or combination of art. It's possible to argue in designing such a response that it would not have been obvious to combine the two or more cited cases, using the nonobvious angle in reverse. Commercial arguments can rely on the notion that no prior solution held as much economic sway as the one now seeking patent protection.

The simple rule of thumb is to include all potential prior art, whether individually compelling or in combination, in your IDS and write your patent application to clearly patent over all of it before filing. Look to the section in Part 2 on prosecution for insight on how to change this part of the conversation.

During prosecution, the interaction is metered by a clock. In reality, it's a one-way street. The examiner can take as much time as needed to create his or her office action. If the action is a rejection and it's not traversed, it will lead to intentional abandonment. And any response from the applicant must be timely made. The office action will stipulate the interval, typically one to three months. Thirty days will apply to technicalities that are easy to correct. Substantive rejections will be permitted a three-month response. If you do give up during prosecution (i.e., do not respond in time to a rejection and do not petition to extend the time for your reply), that is called intentional abandonment. In the preferred situation, the examiner will send a notice of allowance that confirms the patent is in condition for publishing, identifying allowable matter, and pointing out the supporting claim.

Why is this such a cumbersome and painful sequence of events? For one, it is rare that an examiner will identify "matter not shown (i.e., allowable matter)" on the initial examination and therefore not offer allowable notice when first office actions are completed (read that as a rejection). Sometimes the rejection is based on an easily correctable technicality. If it is based on a single piece of art, that's a hard pill to swallow. If it's based on a combination of other pieces of art (i.e., two or more), you may stand a better chance of traversing the rejection. Clearly, if it takes three pieces of prior art to unhook your claimed scope—the probability of you successfully traversing the rejection(s) goes up dramatically.

2.9 International prosecution

It is useful to note that if you file under the PCT, your application will be prosecuted separately by the EPO. You can actually ask that it be prosecuted first. One reason for doing that is that the EPO has a reputation for conducting more complete searches, therefore giving you a more productive prosecution. I will point out here (covered in more detail in the drafting section) that, if you choose expedited filing, you will have to place numbers for all of the elements of your invention into the claim (not only in the detailed description). For European applications, this is required. It is the standard for foreign applications. There is a requirement for using the numbers of any element of the object of invention in the claim itself. For now, just know that prosecution in a foreign office can occur before it occurs in your home country, but most certainly will continue in parallel at some point during prosecution for a global monopoly right.

2.10 Allowed, issued, term, maintenance, and defense

After you have an allowed patent, it can be used even more effectively (marking "patented" as compared to "patent pending") to create a barrier to entry for a competitor, to serve as the basis of a contract or revenue-generating license, or to in some other way contribute to the value of a business—typically considered an intangible asset (check with your accountant on how to treat patents as assets, especially related to expenses and depreciation). When a potential investor or acquiring company sees how to further your or their own business model for commercially exploiting the patent rights, the asset can more readily be ascribed a tangible business value.

Granted utility patents have a maximum term of seventeen years from the date of issue or twenty years from the date of filing (for patent applications filed after June 8, 1995), as long as the required maintenance fees are paid at three and a half, seven and a half, and eleven and a half years following the grant. You get to keep your monopoly during the valid period as long as you have not committed fraud at the patent office and have policed your rights if an interloper seeks to practice any embodiment and markets a product that "reads on an issued claim in your patent." If you licensed them, that's one thing, but if they are operating without your authorization, then you have to deal with it.

If a competitor does use or sell an object of invention covered by your patent, it is your obligation to defend your rights, or you risk losing them. When and how to do this is a delicate dance and can hold great opportunity as well as risk. The use of cease and desist letters applies here, as do declaratory judgments filed by potential defendants. Damages can depend on a number of factors such as if and when an infringer knew they were infringing, whether they did so willfully, and the economic impact of the market conflict. These issues will be highlighted in the sections on business considerations, threats/costs, and patent tactics and strategies.

3.0 More about MPEP fundamentals on patentability and prior art

3.1 Patentability in the context of prior art and the purpose of search

When I first covered patentability, I considered it from the eligibility point of view. This is known as applying MPEP rule 101. It is cut and dried.

As we journey down the utility patenting pathway, you're going to hear a lot more from me about patents that have SCA—that is, patents that have properly scoped claims on the true P-E, for which both the filer and examiner have done complete prior art searches and have found nothing to prevent allowance, enabling the arguments during prosecution to flow without critical objections and permitting the patent to issue with a clean file wrapper.

The discussion here turns on search. There are lots of ways to search. My treatment is not so much about how to search (there are very simple principles on how to do this quickly and smart (get more references on this if you need the how-to's). I'm more concerned with the outcomes and uses of what may be found. Prior art is found by search. As with any part of a process, when you choose to search, how you implement your search for that step in your workflow, and what you do with the art you find is as important as your invention and its P-E.

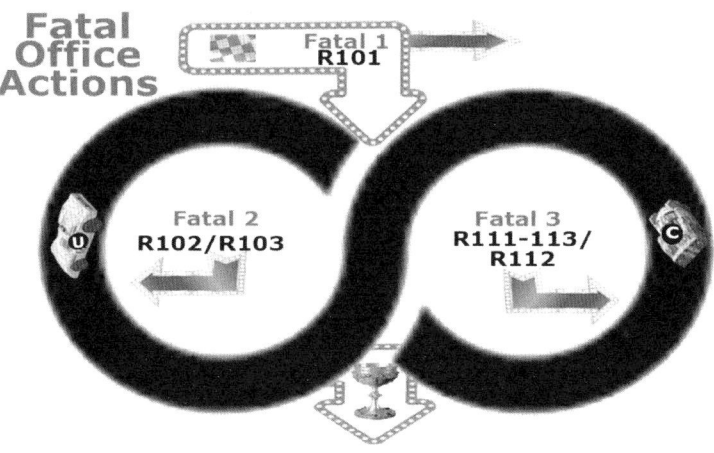

Fig.6 Figure 8 Racetrack MPEP rules on fatal office action rejections (FOARS)

I like to use a racetrack metaphor to convey the sequence of events and timing on how search and interpretation of art will yield a suitable outcome: the holy grail published utility patent. The use of search follows rule 101, eligibility. Search is the basis for forming rule 102 and 103 findings—to confirm or deny novelty (rule 102) and nonobviousness (rule 103). Search will further the conclusions and your representation of enablement (rule 112), and how you unambiguously make all of your antecedent references for the inventive matter are conveyed. You will hear about other rules, including rules 111 and 113, which go toward compliance on the patent's structure and the filing package.

I have pointed out that critical aspects of patentability turn on novelty (this is rule 102) and stipulate that the invention was not anticipated or shown in any prior art. Remember, that said, even if it was not previously known/shown, it must still pass the rule for nonobviousness (rule 103).

You will see that not all searches are created equal. In fact, you will probably hear how a patent search by a US attorney will cost you upward of $3,000 per search. You can go that route, or you can contract with a search firm that utilizes artificial intelligence, get tens of related articles or art, all categorized by the critical terms from the glossary in your draft UCD for service fees of less than $100 an hour. This is one way you can do an assisted search for under $300, all the while keeping your invention a trade secret.

If you are of a mind to, you can do the initial detailed searches yourself using the US Patent Office tools and other free search engines. As a side note, as unadvisable as it is, you can prepare and file your patent application without doing a prior art search and without submitting an IDS, allowing the designated patent office to do the search and make its own determination. This is a bad idea. If this is ever given as guidance, you have to stand firm and just say no.

If you are rejected for rule 103, then it is a case where anyone skilled in the art who would have seen aspects of the proposed invention in those findings might infer your invention is a simple extension of what was known.

A search produces a piece of prior art. If that art is relevant to your P-E, it will serve as a reference (incorporated in your IDS filing as a disclosure that you must explain away). Typical findings are related in some way as stuff that existed before but had egregious limitations. Simply put, a lot of art doesn't show the exact invention, but there is a rub. Art can be combined by the examiner during prosecution as in the notion of two pieces of art "teaching in a direction" of your invention. As a gauge, if you (or the examiner) need three pieces of art to teach your improvement or P-E, then it's likely to pass the nonobvious test rule 103.

For now, I say 95 percent of initial examinations at the patent office will result in an objection and a rejection. Here's the scenario. For rule 103 to be passed allowing the patent application to be further examined on its merits, the invention would have to be nonobvious. The examiner could, and most likely would, combine the related art and impute/infer your invention was obvious by that combination. This would prevent patentability unless traversed during prosecution with plausible arguments on how each of the pieces of art "teaches in different directions."

For now, I want you to think of any prior art as a representation that could undermine rules 102 and 103, so the notion of both novelty and nonobviousness analyses is dual, comingled, and a critical part of your initial assessment about whether to draft. In the IP-BC/ADVANCED and ADVANCED-PRACTITIONER levels, I separate out the intervals in qualifying your P-E for the step of patent drafting, allowing you to make more timely and better determination of rule 102 and 103 rejections. To change the conversation, you can do a lot with well-planned, timely searches, ensuring you develop the layman's claim in your UCD, along with capturing a well-formulated IDS. I call that de-risking your patent draft before filing. This is how you will not only control the patent spend before filing, but also lower prosecution costs after filing. As you can appreciate, these considerations complicate the nature of what is otherwise a simple question—did the invention exist before or not?

Here's another look at why search is a complex part of the utility patenting process. If you are familiar with the childhood behavior study called the "marshmallow test" (if not Google it and have some fun with it), you can see that delaying search just long enough can be a critical factor in how the conversation about whether to patent proceeds. Consider that an inventor can do a search as soon as they think of their invention, without really knowing what their true P-E is and it's unique contribution to the subject matter in the field of art. If an innovator searches too soon, it's easy for an innovator to get functionally fixated on seeing what others have done. This can cloud their intuitive and inspired discovery of elements of their own invention that are truly patentable over the findings. Using the Schwartz Method iterative formulation of a suitable P-E helps delay this discovery just long enough for the inventor to develop their contribution that patents over the other stuff with true clarity.

Another aspect here is if patent counsel asks for your idea too early. They might do this for any one of a number of reasons. Clearly, one ostensible purpose is their goal of filtering and guiding your further efforts before things go too far. Often, at the same time, what they might be doing is beefing up on various forms of enablement in your classification in order to look like the smartest guy in the room. By looking at all of that other art first, they will gain critical insights about your invention's potential without having time to share it with you until their report is done—all at your expense. It is probably clear that the more of this part that you do yourself (but not too early), while acting as if you were the (your own) patent examiner, the better you will be able to convince the rest of the IP hunters on your team, especially patent counsel, that what you have is it, that it really is what you want, and that it is the P-E for the product development steps ahead. At the end of the day, the most important job of counsel needs to be directed at crafting the formal claims as one of the last steps in the process of creating a UCPA. This may be counterintuitive but think about it. The only time you need to worry about legalese in the actual final claim is when the patent draft (see the drafting section) has reached what we call a UCD, not what the patent counsel typically calls an invention disclosure (the general description of your invention). More on this later.

It gets even more involved if art was known and not disclosed at the time of filing or found before actual examination and after filing. In best practice, your prior art search should be progressively documented and archived as part of your trade secrets, tagged with your analysis. When the time is right, another step at the end of drafting and just before preparing your filing package would to document the most critical findings you want to show as patenting over and include them in your IDS. There, you identify each piece of key art and explain how your invention patents over that stuff. The reason for diligently doing this (preparation) is to anticipate and halo any examination interpretations that otherwise may result in perfunctory rejections on rules 102 and 103. Know that if any art is later found, unintentionally and unavoidably by the inventor or anyone on the cohort team, while your application is pending, it must be submitted to the patent office immediately.

A worse situation is when art you did not use is found by another after you filed, and intentionally used by a competitor in a petition (one of various kinds) to either preempt examination on what you thought were the merits by apprising the patent office of the art for a published but yet-to-be-examined application, have an allowance withdrawn if it hasn't issued and published yet, or, even harsher, seek to have your issued patent invalidated.

In at least one other circumstance, you and a competitor can have your patent applications in the patent office at the same time, each with other, additional art, which was independently and severally discovered. Just like outside counsel does when accepting you as a client, a due diligence investigation is done at the patent office before taking your case on as an examination so that examiners are not representing competitors in the same technology space. The patent office does an internal investigation in the art group to see if any other patent examiner is conterminously examining a like or similar invention from someone else. If there are two equivalent patents in the patent office at the same time, this would result in an interference proceeding. If you each used different but related prior art in your applications, that art would be merged and applied to each of your cases. The examiners use this investigation to collaborate and determine who has claim rights, remembering that the one whose filing is dated first will have the priority. If theirs prevails over all of the art from both applications, that will be a big win. The additional art will be listed on the allowed patent by the examiner. In the old days, before AIA, interference disputes were resolved based on the first proven date of conception. Now, the decision is simplified by just looking at the first filing date.

No matter if your inventions are substantively different and don't directly read on each other, the art in your IDS might still be used to unhook a competing patent application or vice versa and result in one or the other being allowed and granted the patent irrespective of who filed first. Every case has its unique spin. So doing a complete sequence of progressively deeper search dives along your pathway (see guidance on best practices for when to search in IP-BC) will increase your likelihood of getting a patent issued with properly scoped claims. When you are issued a patent with a clean file wrapper that supports your claims over any competitor, you will have a patent with what I call SCA—the patent withstands the test of time (during and after) for all prior art known, found, or applied. Patents like this cannot be readily invalidated on the basis of rules 102 and 103. This does not ensure proof of life, as you will see when we consider rules 111, 112, and 113 that ensure the story in your specification is told in compliance with MPEP requirements.

The point of these initial use cases is to highlight the at least four players in the search process when pursuing utility patents: (1) you as innovator during conception, (2) patent counsel as drafter during preparation and for filing, (3) the examiner during prosecution, and (4) competitors on/after/or even before publishing (as in the case of the eighteen-month rule). Make sure you understand some of the new, after allowance, streamlined petitions now available to question your rights at the patent office. I cover this in the patent tactics and strategies section later on.

Each of these participants has a different goal at a different time, using prior art as a critical component of their decision-making process. It is important to understand that under all four points of view, as well as in any other scenarios I depict, an underlying principle is at play. The principle, originally referred to as the mythical man (now I hasten to say mythical man or woman) holds that this person theoretically knows every element of prior art in the field and has that art at their fingertips when evaluating and applying their search/art discovery in the assessment of patentability for rules 102 and 103.

Whether you are making a go/no-go call or drafting an IDS compilation to establish your case for novelty and nonobviousness with the examiner, your implicit obligation is to do the hard work of proving your innocence, even though you are innocent until proven guilty. During prosecution, the examiner is ultimately seeking to clear his desk, for better or worse.

Other use cases abound. In each situation, your analysis must be focused and mindful. When a competitor is seeking to nullify your monopoly rights, there may be an infringement case (or not). You may be seeking to establish your right or freedom to operate if someone else tries to stop you by asserting their claimed rights. It's all fair play, and you need to know what you're doing each step of the way. Just know that in the heat of battle, there will always be such a mythical know-it-all. Think of it this way. The closest approximation to that mythical know-it-all is accomplished by someone with the greatest self-interest in what is called a "slow grind search." Searches like this can be conducted over an extended period of time by anyone, for any one of a number of reasons. Just know that if there is art out there that is relevant to the scope of your claims, and you have an invention of real commercial value. That art will be found and applied against you, so find it first and determine if it is a deal breaker.

Search is your friend if you know when and how to use it to find prior art, understand its potential, know its limits, and know how to use it as an accelerant on your pathway to patentship. It's not counterintuitive to try to break your own patentable idea early, even for the inventor who may think there's no way his or her invention existed before. Sometimes innovators underestimate their own inventiveness.

3.2 More on prior art: Rule 102: Public disclosure—engagement with others

It is a simple truth that the earlier in your process you know that there is something out there that can destroy the novelty of your invention in others' eyes (examiner, competitor), it should be used as a decision point on whether to proceed with drafting, filing, and persisting in prosecuting that application at a patent office. I cover this when I discuss the file wrapper: how it will expose any flaws in your application during prosecution and how it will become a public document that publishes with your application if allowed. If you can bully an examiner to issue (it's done every day), using weak arguments to traverse rejections for 102 and 103, woe be the day. You don't want to fall into that trap—ever.

By way of summary, and without fear of repeating myself: anything that came before your invention is referred to as prior art. It is a prior reference in one of many forms not limited to a patent, a printed publication such as an article, a book, a website, a white paper, or knowledge about the public use or sale of an object comprising the claimed elements of your P-E. It is relevant in some way to the claim in your patent for your invention. It can or may have occurred in any classification of art and it can be from anywhere in the world. The point that there might be related technology classes where an invention like yours might have had utility suggests that clever search is not limited to your own direct/immediate art field. Here you really have to think outside the box to ensure your search scope is aligned with your innovation.

The one year rule revisited: for the US Patent Office, since the United States is now operating under the AIA, making it a first-to-file nation for any patent applications filed on or after March 16, 2013, there is a grace period. This is a restatement of the one-year rule: If you make your own public disclosure or publication, you have twelve months to file your patent application claiming your invention in the United States. Just know that since the United States now has a first-to-file system, if someone else publicly discloses your invention details before you get your filing date for your patent application, it can and will be considered prior art against your patent application when the examiner is assessing your novelty. In simple terms, establishing novelty is a race against time. This is why I employ the racetrack metaphor when explaining my view of FOARs.

If the invention has already been or is about to be shared, you need to look at the form in which it is being disclosed. If engaged with others, are you operating with or without a nondisclosure/confidentiality agreement? If you're about to publish in print, electronically, or in some other form such as a blog post made available to any outside, you better have filed a provisional application at a minimum, and any such disclosure will trigger the one-year rule for filing your non-provisional application. It's a good habit to track these dates on a master calendar along with marking critical future dates—that is, one year out (it's good to automate this with alerts, but I found that an old-school, multiyear visual calendar, color-coded by application, worked best, especially when building a patent portfolio. If you're not careful, you will become your own prior art. Always record the name, company/agency, date, place, and circumstances of any disclosure and plan accordingly. Remember, as soon as the invention is sold or offered for sale, whether or not an actual sale occurred, the one-year rule will be triggered. You will also be at risk in any effort you may have to file internationally. The one-year rule is one of the most critical triggers for your IP workflow, so the key is using your improved utility patenting processes to avoid being forced to rush an application.

You can see the importance of keeping your invention as a trade-secret until you file. Keep disclosures to others secret by having them sign a confidentiality or nondisclosure agreement. Do this, if you can, in order to protect your ability to file abroad and to prevent the start of your twelve-month grace period. At the same time, this may not be possible. Why? When you are working with a patent attorney, they are bound by attorney-client privilege (patent agents may not be so bound, so be cautious), however, if you are partnering, which could take the form of licensing or another instrument, in most cases those companies will have anti-confidentiality clauses and won't sign yours. Their reasoning is simple—they might already be working on it and be preparing their own patent application. If anything, you might actually hasten their filing by suggesting you have something like what they're doing.

Outside of the United States, most countries require that you file a patent application describing your invention before publication or public disclosure. If you break this rule, you will become your own prior art there, and you will be barred from getting a patent application in those countries. If you file and try to evade the 1-year rule by not disclosing your trigger event, that's fraud. If you miss your one-year window, you will have permanently lost your right to make claims for that invention.

3.3 When you search in other fields of art

"Matter" is classified into specific categories, and any piece of relevant art is applicable, independent of its classification or field of use. Such art can be the basis for denying patentability under rules

102 and 103. So, for example, say you invented a hinge for manipulating a computing surface and classified it as factoring in computer hardware (like I did, and I called it a "surface" in my first claim of my first patent in 1989). If that hinge existed before on a bus door in the transportation classification, or as a binding for a book a pilot might use in the tight cockpit of an airplane (in either flight management or in binders), that can and will be used against your claimed invention. If you invented a new kind of backpack and searched in hiking gear but did not search in clothing, you might get a rude awakening: a finding that your invention read on a prior patent on an article of clothing that incorporated your inventive object. You have to think broadly when you consider the ways in which your invention might be repurposed for utility/applicability and use. If you search too narrowly, it could come back and bite you since good examiners understand this process very well—and, trust me, you want to look like your own good examiner during preparation, and also pray you get a great one for your examination. There's nothing worse than finding out your patent can be invalidated downstream after a notice of allowance.

3.4 More on when prior art is used, how it is used, and where it is used

Enough can't be said on prior art. When you decide to proceed with a prior art search, you can do it yourself or you can have it done using a professional searching service. As suggested, the inventor or a cohort IP hunter should do their own searching first.

To me, what this means is very different than what you might hear or be told about when and how to do this. In IP-BC, I am clear that this first search should be done at the end of INTERVAL 1, as instructed during the IP-BC/ADVANCED-PRACTITIONER level, when you have your initial layman's claim: the preferred language and terms that detail your innovation, along with a glossary and figures/drawings with those terms and arrows applied to the figures (no numbers yet). In this way, you will drill into stuff that is more relevant sooner than later, before you engage other outsiders. You should create a digital file directory and categorize the findings as they relate to the different parts of what you intend to claim.

You may be told to provide a basic description of your invention to someone, to be searched on as in a "one-page description with a figure." When you hear that, be wary because when you engage a professional patent lawyer as your searcher, the cost can range from $1,000 to $3,000 per invention searched and analyzed. The operative word that ties to cost is "analyzed." If you follow my IP SAVVYS prescription, you will do the analysis every day as part of your trade secret program. There may be a time to invoke a mythical person in a slow grind search, or not. If you really know your invention, you will know when to search and what to make of the findings, without anyone else engaged in the process.

When considering the how-to's of search, it's important to know that this is a very well-understood process, completely taught and documented at the US Patent Office and elsewhere. Becoming good at this yourself is part of the hard work you must do if you're serious about utility patenting. Find any one of the guides on how to do it, starting at the US Patent Office. There, you will want to note the target databases provided. One database is the allowed and issued/published patents database, and the other is the pending patent applications database with cases that have been published based on the eighteen-month rule. Remember that this latter database is the one where the application is placed and published globally eighteen months after filing if you didn't stipulate that the patent would not be filed internationally on filing in your home country. Here are other search tools you may use: the Internet, Google's Patent and Prior Art search engines, free patents online, and international patents at various publishers.

You may be told that a good time to search is when you are asked to provide a one-page invention disclosure to your patent professional at the time they propose an official engagement to prepare your patent application. See notes on this above—no. In any engagement, you will want to advise counsel (especially outside counsel) that you only want to trigger billable events on your definition of the work and that it be only for substantive work, and further that no work is authorized unless and until approved by you, especially for situations where a relevant patent might be found, and before "analysis." You want to do all initial analyses.

You may be told that you're about to break the one-year rule and there isn't sufficient time to search before filing, in which case you should file a provisional application and then perform your search before your non-provisional application. This is not a very good idea under any circumstances. Usually, the suggested provisional application is crafted (note I did not say drafted) without a claim and the terms that describe the P-E and its inventive step, ill defined. Even if a quick search can still be performed as a last-minute qualifier, any search using that document as part of the invention disclosure's conversion to a patent application will be misguided and expensive and will ultimately not result in a filing that enables you to reach your goal. The early and continuous search you do while making yourself the mythical person will allow you to manage this conversation.

You may be told how important it is to keep your patent professional in the know with every aspect of your work during the development of your invention. Not exactly—if you want to own and control the process and keep the costs under control, you will restructure your IP workflow to consult with counsel for only substantive issues. This is actually good for both of you. You will know when and what to ask for, and the legal invoices will be targeted, make sense, and ensure that they are timely paid. In the IP-BC course, I provide clear decision points in utility patenting workflows for when to engage outside resources, what tasks to define, and what completed work to expect. When you know them, you can reduce your patent spending by up to 70 percent, improve the quality of your patent applications, and file more patent applications.

3.5 Search and prior art: Other places where it fits in

I have identified that search factors into a variety of steps in the acquisition and maintenance of a patent portfolio. These other applications of search shape up as analysis. There are different names for these functional searches. Examples include chain-of-ownership searches (think the registry of deeds for real estate property), white-space analysis in a crowded field of invention (finding gaps in the field for your utility), patentability (novelty/nonobviousness) searches by you (as discussed already, the examiner and your competitors), infringement/noninfringement opinions, proof of life or validity opinions, and freedom-to-operate opinions.

Know that there can't be an alleged infringement/noninfringement or a need to establish freedom to operate unless and until there are competing allowed, issued, and published claimed patents and/

or products that read on the claims in those patents, whether they are yours or your competitor's.

At some point you may be told that there is an alleged infringement of your patent and that you will need to have an infringement/noninfringement opinion. Before you freak out, make your own analysis before engaging in any expensive process. Look at the alleged offending thing, take it apart if you can, read the patent (if there is one, find out its filing date), using the Schwartz Method to reverse engineer your own examination of it. Do all of that before you jump the gun. Do the same thing if you get a cease and desist letter that alleges you're an infringer. Something may be similar but patently different, and not even bother you at all. In fact, it may be good for the market, allowing customers to see alternatives and make choices. Sometimes, the more the merrier.

You may have to establish your rights affirmatively to keep your patents valid (defend them) or establish that you did not willfully infringe if a case is made against you. One thing that is done to defend a patent against infringement is to write a letter to the infringer. This is a critical event, and it can trigger a "declaratory judgment" countersuit in the state in which the infringer is operating their business—a lawsuit against you and opposing your allegations. There are many points to consider before sending such a letter, so be very sure before you send such a letter. Remember that triple damages may result if you knowingly or intentionally infringe someone's claimed invention embodied in a product that is being made, used, or sold.

You may be told that one way to avoid the accusation of patent infringement is to simply invalidate the accusing patent holder's issued patent. "Breaking a patent" is an entire field populated by professionals who do this day in and day out. They act like bounty hunters as they attempt to find new prior art references that were not considered by you or the patent examiner when the patent at issue was granted. Someone will pay them if they find something "good" to break your patent. With the new *ex parte* procedures, anyone seeking to invalidate your published patent can do so at far less expense than under prior rules and costs to oppose an issued patent so as to invalidate it. Part of the reason for this is that patent offices are overwhelmed, so they structure procedures to augment their examination and they welcome any crowdsourced dimensions as a way to continuously police patents and weed out the "bad ones." A bit more on this is included in the section on patent strategy. Also, as a member of IP-BC, you can check the blog on my website, ipboostcamp.com, and read the posts on ex parte petitions.

3.6 How to change the conversations on your pathway to patentship

In the previous three sections, I covered the fundamentals of MPEP in no-legalese language meant for everyone to understand, not only the patent counsel shamans but also the CEO's and innovators at technology centric companies. There is nothing here that patent counsel would disagree with. The point of Part 1 is to make sure that there is a common understanding among all parties in the IP hunt about what's at stake and the rules under which the patent hunt will be run. In revealing this framework as simply as possible, I try to expose the doors you will need to open on the patenting pathway as well as who is behind them and the implicit goals and objectives of the "combatants". I promised that the purpose of Part 2 is to ferret out the truths and myths about the critical events and decision points on your pathway to patentship, down the IP corridor of uncertainty. Here, my goal is to share nuances about the nature of each door you will open, more about who's behind those door, and the potentially conflicting objectives each person might have, and how they will seek to steer the utility patent conversation. When you understand the MPEP framework detailed in Part 1, the turning points for all of your conversations will make more sense and your ability to change arguments into collaboration will be enhanced. Take the next step in understanding how to improve your patenting outcomes. This will take a little discipline as you integrate the ideas behind my universal patenting language (UPL) and guiding principles (GP). This would be a good time to take a quick look at the appendix to review the basic ideas underlying the Schwartz Method (TSM) and how they will play into your utility patenting workflow. As a pointer to a fundamental consideration, I will reassert the idea that my patenting language is consistent and compliant with MPEP. I also reassert that my patenting language is equivalent to that used by patent counsel with one crucial caveat. This caveat is most readily disclosed when you try to reconcile patent counsels ask for an "invention disclosure document" and TSM's ask for an "invention disclosure patent application workbook entry (IDPAW entry)". Why? Because the primary difference is not in the semantics but in the grammar of the formulation. In an invention disclosure you provide answers to a set of questions about your invention without any insight into how they will be used to formulate a patent draft. With IDPAW's, I elicit not only the questions you must answer, but show you how to iteratively incorporate them into a representation that is utility patent compliant, section by section. You will see the underlying rubric of how a patent is created is interleaved into the IDPAW so that every compete entry aligns with your P-E's product development roadmap.

This might seem like a lot to integrate, and many will defer to patent counsel early in the patent drafting process because of what might have seemed to be the overwhelming complexity of the mission. If you want to be IP SAVVY and really do it almost all yourself, you can if you will. If you choose the IP SAVVYS model for utility patenting, you will be able to self-manage your workflow, save money, increase patent application quality, speed up the drafting, and reduce the risk of a flawed prosecution that results in a messy file wrapper and a weak if not lost patent effort. So, take a run through the appendix and glossary, then do Part 2 justice, and it will return the investment with unexpected rewards.

PART 2 Changing your utility patenting conversation with The Schwartz Method (TSM)

4.0 Changing your Utility Patenting Conversation

4.1 Changing your IP conversation: Changing what? With whom? How?

The entire IP-BC online course is designed to give you the framework and methods for changing your IP conversation about everything utility patent. So, for each of the steps outlined in Part 1, there are preferred ways to deal with the before, during, and after phases of converting an idea into a patent. This means you should learn a solid UPL along with a GP framework that make patenting into an engineering science, and you should find the best way to apply that new knowledge to your pathway to patentship. If you take the IP SAVVYS approach, you will have that discipline combined with new, different, and better conversations about drafting, prosecution, and commercialization. Let's see how all of this can play out.

As in any good story, if it's possible to use a metaphor to explore an idea use it. Alan Kaye said years back, a picture is worth a thousand words, but a metaphor is worth a thousand pictures. In all of the descriptive matter delivered here in this book and in my online course, I try to hold true to that paradigm for explaining how to get utility patents with sustainable competitive advantage.

Assuredly, you will engage with patent counsel at one point or another as you open each door along the IP corridor of uncertainty, and at each point the conversation will be different. At the end of the day, to be organized in pursuit of utility patents, everyone needs to use the same language and guiding principles—otherwise it's chaos.

A magic pill that organizes both IP Counsel & Innovator?

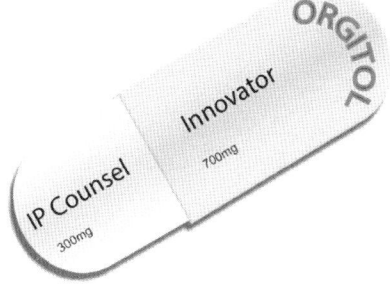

Fig.7 Let IP SAVVYS approach be your orgitol pill for both innovator and patent counsel

Not only do you want to avoid chaos, but I assure you your patent counsel doesn't want chaos either. By getting on the same page, you will accelerate down the utility patenting learning curve together. Here's how we think about this book: make IP SAVVYS method the orgitol capsule that organizes both innovator and counsel.

Any part of the conversation is comprised of complex talking points. What if both innovator and IP counsel took a magic potion that got them organized with a newfound love? (Vignette #1, https://www.ipboostcamp.com). Since each person has a different set of utility patent goals and objectives, they will experience unique conversations with utility patent experts that have differing understandings, skill sets, and motivations. I seek to offer an organized point of view and language that aligns these conversations and turns an otherwise ad hoc process into a mutually organized and highly productive one. Even if some part of what I share here is familiar, I guarantee the more you know about the Schwartz Method and BBT, the easier it will be to change the IP conversation you are having with others in the IP hunt, forever and for the better. Using our UPL and GP, you can turn your IP pathway to patentship from a walk of shame or a walk of pain into a walk of fame.

The key idea in changing the IP conversation about utility patenting is keeping you out of the "argument room" as you open each door (covered in my IP-BC online course with a video clip in the starter-kit Monty Python vignette called "Worth the Price of Admission").

4.2 The nature of the conversation

Everyone's IP goals are different, so there is no one conversation about utility patenting. However, there are some fundamentals that will guide you. If everyone gets it—that is, is IP savvy, then the considerations and conversations should be like the Mona Lisa smile, seen in more or less the same way, even though viewed from different angles. In this vignette, the idea of GP can be made more clearly. GP represents the values.

**Strangers in a strange land...
Is it really only about the language?**

Fig.8 Pathway to patentship and GP as the values

When immigrants arrive at the Statue of Liberty, not only do they make a choice to speak a common language, but they also share a set of common values. In my effort to develop the contents of this book and the accompanying course, IP-BC, I advocate for and deliver a common UPL for drafting utility patents, along with a set of GP rules on how to draft a patent using the Schwartz Patent Rubric. This is covered as Vignette #2, https://www.ipboostcamp.com. Using this framework, having a readily shared "grammar" and "semantic rules" all can agree on, offers a pathway to patentship in a similar way to how the English language and the values of the US Constitution offer a pathway to US citizenship.

Summarizing, the key idea here is to get everyone into the IP Zone. You can think about the IP Zone in at least two ways. One is the macro point of view. In this view, a company's business interests hinge on the interests of its people within the ecosystem in which they are commercially engaged.

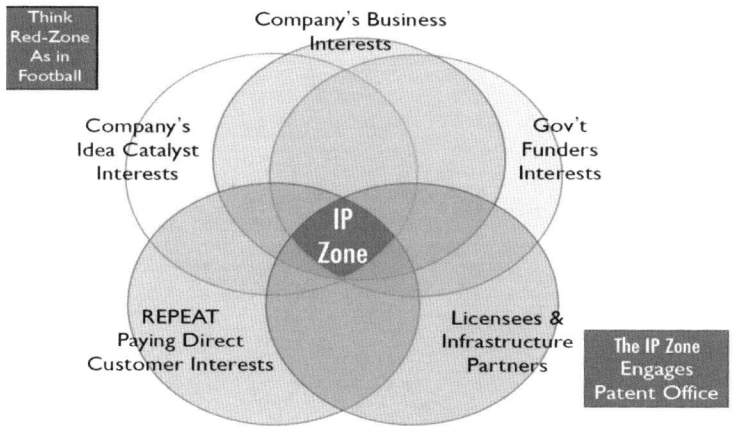

Fig 9. The IP Zone as a Venn diagram of intersecting interests

In the second view, you can map out the goals of the people and see how their deeper interests, IP roles, and tasking create a framework with complex and competing objectives that need to be in dynamic stability for it to function.

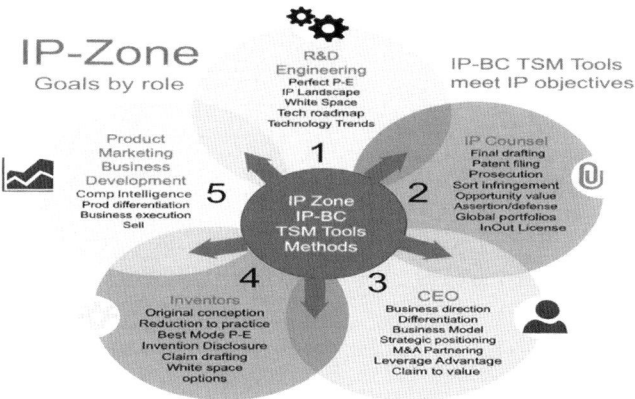

Fig.10 The IP Zone as the intersection of mutual goals and objectives of IP cohorts

The innovator/inventor runs up the stairs every day with a vision and intentions to change the world. Patent counsel seeks to be his or her able-bodied assistant in securing the monopoly rights that a patent confers (the kingmaker). Much as in any relationship, the more you mindfully share with one another, the more likely you will be to succeed. At the same time, there are some clear turning points where the choice of what to say and who to say it to will impact your utility patenting quality and speed. In reprocessing this guide, I seek to inform and enlighten future IP conversations by helping identify the goals and objectives of each hunter and what part of the patenting jigsaw puzzle they are tasked to solve. Their roles may or may not match their titles, but after rationalizing the IP workflows using our UPL and GP, some of that may change too as you rethink who does what, when, and how.

Turning points with patent counsel have triggers that are more urgent and riskier. Those conversations are the most critical. I point out numerous dimensions of this in what follows. For example, if you are about to do a public disclosure of critical elements of your P-E, you will trigger a bunch of things on the patenting pathway, not to mention the one-year rule. This will also raise an alarm for securing international rights. But let's not get ahead of ourselves or confuse and strike fear in hearts by identifying risks, tactics, and strategies until we have covered the fundamental truths. Then you can use those truths to make more informed choices at each step.

4.3 Reminder: Truths, trade-offs, and the before-during-after approach

There are many, many considerations in pursuing a utility patent or portfolio, among them MPEP rules, issues of ownership, language when drafting and finalizing claims and filing, timing, use and role of prior art, explicit US Patent Office requirements for submission, prosecution sequences for the patent application and its file wrapper, the scope of allowances, and post-publication and post-issuance considerations. These considerations need to be tempered by threats, costs, and business considerations.

Fig. 11 Misconceptions: Myths vs Facts

By separating truths from trade-offs, I seek to enable mutual understanding about the reality of preparing and filing utility patents at the lowest cost. I hold onto this consistently throughout this book and my course. There are numerous additional postings on my blog about these considerations for members of the course (https://www.ipboostcamp.com/blog).

Another approach to telling the truth without being an alarmist is delivered in how I sort out the phases, keeping to the before, during, and after approach in telling the conversion story, making things clearer and ensuring you are better informed. How you engage others with these insights will determine your unique IP conversations. During each complex conversation, keep Schwartz on your shoulder, "fly your helicopter up 1000', and look down at yourself." This will be the most mindful way to integrate all of the points of view at play in your IP landscape.

A fundamental guiding principle is the Schwartz Patent Rubric. It derives from what a patent looks like in the MPEP representation. In principle, they are one and the same, because if there was any difference, then what I am sharing would not serve to get a utility patent on file that can be examined on its merits and allowed with published patent rights. Simply, the Schwartz Patent Rubric is the secret sauce on how to understand the internal semantics of a patent allowing you to separate the creation of one from the section by section formatting of one. It comprises the Schwartz Method, which is the way a patent is constructed. It includes universal definitions for each part of what is inside your patent along with semantics for all of the interdependencies among the patent sections. It is comprised of a set of iterative steps that ensures the elements that should be constructed first are represented first. It provides a simple order of creation, permitting clarity for each patenting milestone, at the lowest cost and with the minimal things needed to move onto the next milestone. This sequence is the formation of a utility-compliant disclosure (UCD) followed by a utility-compliant patent application (UCPA).

Basically, the Schwartz Method defines and ensures the formulation of a UCD that can be rapidly converted into an MPEP organized, non-provisional patent application. This is the game-changer in the IP conversations that will follow. In summary, the Schwartz Method and Schwartz Patent Rubric offer mechanics for drafting a patent application that is airtight, right the first time, and de-risked from fatal rejections before filing. It is designed to ensure that during the prosecution phase, you can get to the heart of allowable subject matter for publication at the lowest cost and in the most efficient manner. For this reason, we separate out the mechanics of the Schwartz Method into the drafting section. Once you review and understand what a patent is, then and only then do I provide guidance on how to draft one. If you know all of the MPEP fundamentals already, skim and/or skip this section and you will not be in the fog when we move into the sections where the Schwartz Method drafting guidelines are shared.

Since I provide the critical staging for each of the iterative steps in fleshing out and specifying the P-E for a utility patent specification, I can offer my 85 percent/15 percent rule about patent construction: 85 percent of what is drafted is subject matter independent and follows a core protocol that ensures de-risking for FOARs before filing, and 15 percent is the nuanced aspects of enablement in the classification for your inventive matter. In the IP-BC/ENTRY level of my course, there is a short video clip with further explanation and a Venn diagram that makes this even clearer. The IP-BC/INTERMEDIATE level of the course dives into this GP rule in even more detail. The ADVANCED and ADVANCED-PRACTITIONER levels teach how to apply the rule with your own IP.

What is helpful in the full course is that I dissect the need to know and apply the Schwartz Method into a set of levels based on the IP role and tasking for each player in the IP hunt. Separating out these critical utility patenting considerations in this way, users (from CEO to innovator and everywhere in between) can gain insight into who is responsible for each part of this critical job of ensuring the target invention for your patent application passes the bar on patentability. Further, with this mutual understanding and trust, you will be better able to streamline your IP workflows as you self-manage your utility patenting processes in what I call the DIAAY system of IP tasking.

Accepting my premise on UPL and GP, let's dig into the sequence of phases in utility patenting and the nature of better conversations and how to get them working for you in your pursuit of the holy grail: an SCA utility patent. Our approach is all about getting patent counsel and the patent office to work for you.

5.0 Changing the utility patenting conversation starts with drafting airtight patents

5.1 Drafting with the Schwartz Method (TSM)

It's important to understand that in the same sense as writing a great novel, there is a tried-and-true formula for constructing a classic read. In the novel, there is a point of view, a setting, a complication, a turning point, and a resolution. This is all developed in such a way as to incorporate the key characters with all of their blessings and foibles. However, the essence of a great classic is the interdependencies, the nonlinear creation formulation. This is how the story(line) is created, using inference techniques like flashbacks, and so forth—the rubric of any author and how the story is told is what makes the author's technique work and is what ultimately makes the book compelling enough to sell. In this sense, writing is a creative art. Patent counsel would have you believe that when creating a patent story, it is an abstract and creative art. In point of fact, it doesn't have to be. Of course, a great patent counsel drafter can get it right, in the end, while having a field day in the process of creating their version of your story in their version of your patent application. For the great patent counsel authors, all the more power to them, and good luck finding the right one for your field of classification and your inventive matter.

Changing the conversation: Here, the goal is not to diminish the work of great patent counsel, but rather to turn the patent drafting process into an engineering science where at least 15 percent of the story is developed as an integral part of the product engineering process, and 85 percent of the story is a plug-in. The essence of this is the underlying framework of the patent rubric delivered in the Schwartz Method. You're not ready to change the drafting conversation quite yet. It is my purpose here to share what I mean by the UPL and GP. When you get your arms around that, then and only then will you be in control of the theme of the story and in charge of the patent drafting conversation.

5.2 What is the Schwartz Method

As explained in the section on what a patent is (true at all patent offices), a tried-and-true structure is required for filing. Rather than an art form (as some would have you believe), the patent rubric is the interweave of each of the sections in a repeatably constructible form. For this reason, with Schwartz, I liken it to an engineering discipline. In the Schwartz Method drafting technique, you I convey the simple notion that the order of delivery (the tried-and-true required structure) is not the order of creation. Once you understand this aspect of the Schwartz Patent Rubric (with your IP, especially the P-E of your invention comprising your novel enablement), everything else will fall into place in a heartbeat. This is not to diminish the required elements of a formal patent application with it's clear and definite presentation. The order of delivery is what is required under rule 111 when you file at the patent office. Leave anything out, and the filing package will be rejected without any examination.

In order to put TSM in perspective, It is helpful to understand the different states or stages that an idea traverses on its way to becoming a patent application. It's also helpful to remind ourselves of the old days under the first-to-invent system. In those days, the way inventors established their date of conception was to use something called a document disclosure procedure (not the "invention disclosure document asked for by most patent counsel). Using this procedure, an inventor sent themselves a sealed, certified (general) description of their idea (usually in a very rough form as might have been copied out of their invention notebook). They did this in order to establish their date of conception and potential ownership rights, downstream following allowance. The sequence of these snapshots of lab notebook entries, descriptive but not structured in any form of a patent draft, and without any claims, would be used in a compilation. Often this document package would become part of the counsel's requested invention disclosure or would be filed as a provisional without any claims. Once handed to a patent counsel in this amorphous state, it would start the patent counsel's drafting process. This old-school way of capturing IP is the crux of the problem, not only for creating patents with quality, but doing it at the lowest possible cost. Yes, back then, if you archived your inventive disclosures in a secure way, you might be able to establish the earliest date of conception for what ultimately is a filed and issued patent. More often than not, while evolving claim scope for the anticipated rights, up until the last minute, it would always necessitate adding new matter to describe the P-E, which would start the drafting process over with counsel. This all might seem sketchy at best, but often inventions were perfected in such a way that they could be used in a court of law, if need be, to prove first conception for the claimed object of invention. Not any longer, IP SAVVY one.

With the Schwartz Method, you will create three critical sections of the IDPAW with each iteration. An IDPAW entry will at a minimum be comprised of at least one figure of the P-E known to the inventor at that time, a glossary with the terms for the elements of that embodiment (not numbered-just named and identified by function), a layman's English language claim for it, and a working description of how that P-E works. Since each of these iterations is tied in with either an actual product development step or a mental version of what that next P-E would be to make it the best version of itself, you are essentially drafting a patent internally, as part of your lab notebook entry, without engaging counsel, without spending any money on outside resources, and without divulging that you have to anyone except your key cohorts with a need to know. You will find the details of how this works, step by step, in the IP-BC course levels. The most detailed elements of TSM are included in ADVANCED and ADVANCED-PRACTITIONER. The most important take away for now is that TSM is the antidote for what counsel asks for as an invention disclosure. Not only does the IDPAW entry include the required elements, but more importantly, when you reach the stage when you believe you have the P-E down, you can add the other elements of the IDPAW to complete the story, create your UCD, and even turn that into a UCPA. If you update your entry with the rest of the information I elicit, not limited to the background and the explanation of how you patent over the egregious limitations of the known prior art, you're on your way to avoiding a black hole during drafting. Use the glossary explanation for more details on this and take the ADVANCED level with the coupon offered to sort it out and put it into practice.

5.2 If you have a patentable invention, how and when should you engage outside counsel?

When do you start drafting a patent application with a professional patent attorney? If you unravel this question, the first step in answering is to determine whether you have something that is eligible and patentable (novel and unobvious).

Let's set aside the request by counsel for an invention disclosure document. That term is an anathema and is not actually in the TSM vernacular. As explained, I have a the IDPAW entry with much more sensible and richer properties. You will also find that my UCD is the preferred way to communicate inventive matters. In the glossary you will be able to find more details on this and how the UCD and UCPA are the key conversation changers for the IP SAVVY players.

Changing the conversation: You may be told that as soon as you have a patentable idea it should be discussed with a patent professional using their version of an invention disclosure template. In their request, they will probably ask you about the prior art you have already found, whether in a competing company's product or as another patent or article. They will be doing their best to assess whether your invention has potential and is patentable. Part of what they might ask (or what an invention website might ask) includes your answers to a bunch of questions about what you're trying to do.

The conversation changing point here is that these questions and your iterative answers to them should be in the iterative capture and archiving of critical, differentiating properties of your invention, and they should well be kept trade secrets unless and until you are sure about the object of your P-E and your intention to proceed with a patent application. What you will want to consider in your internal evaluation is answers to the following set of questions. With TSM you will be answering these questions with progressive completions of the IDPAW entries. Here are some of the questions about the properties of your P-E that you should have in your lab notebook entries for each iteration in your invention process. The answers will continue to change for the better. When they stop changing, you will be at a decision point about drafting or not.

(1) What was the state of the art prior for your invention at the point of your conception? What was the preexisting problem, and how was it solved before your invention?

(2) What is the closest inventive matter, marketing collateral, webpages, devices, preexisting methods, that might solve the same problem you are solving but in a different way that delivers #1? In this context, is there a specific company you would be competing with using your solution?

(3) If you could construct a combination of previously known elements that are similar to your invention, would that produce your inventive step or yield unexpected behavior?

(4) What is the unique quality of your invention?

(5) What sources would you explore to find more of these art elements? What are they? (6) Can you identify the industry where companies might have related problem-solving products?

In summary, since the document disclosure procedure is no longer supported nor would it be as critical under the current first-to-file system, you need to sort out the best mode of your P-E with supported claims. Getting there is no cakewalk. You may be told, when you are moving the state of your invention from the idea stage to a more formal depiction, that you should fill out that invention disclosure document. That is a horse of an entirely different color. Usually, a template is provided along with a set of elements to fill in, which will allow an attorney to begin patent drafting. Here, a word to the wise is in line. In IP-BC we direct the process in what is a self-management sequence of events to create a UCD. This is a much stronger depiction of your invention, and it's got the essence of the true invention, in its best mode, as a constrained and enabled P-E. That's our minimum jumping-off point for a dialogue with patent counsel.

Changing the conversation: You may be told that once you have collected your answers you should give them to your patent professional so they can prepare to draft a patent application covering your invention. The sequence of events leading up to your formulation of a UCD would suggest otherwise. In the IP-BC/ADVANCED-PRACTITIONER level, you will build your layman's version of your invention and give yourself all of the critical parameters to answer these questions internally before engaging any patent counsel. The database of art you find as you iterate on your P-E and the definitions of its best mode will allow you to explain away these findings (remaining positive and never diminishing your invention or its component parts), providing the basis for one of the most important documents that will accompany your UCD, the IDS.

For our purpose here, I emphasize the essence of drafting a patent application that inevitably will result in a document that follows the structure of a patent as required at the patent office (rule 113) for filing. Don't confuse what you are encouraged to provide as an invention disclosure document with the Schwartz Method UCD. They intend to enable one and the same thing, but the UCD is a much more well-defined depiction that can be automatically translated into a non-provisional utility patent application. That is what IP-BC is all about, and this is what is taught in the ADVANCED and ADVANCED-PRACTITIONER levels.

5.3 How are you going to get there? Invention disclosure document vs. utility compliant disclosure vs. draft patent application vs. provisional vs. non-provisional patent application

What are you going to try to convey in a finally drafted patent application?

Make no mistake about it—the only thing that matters in the end are the claims you make in the patent application that you file.

The "claims" section of a patent comes at the end of the patent application. As previously explained, claims are in the form of numbered run-on sentences that use an MPEP-based form of expression, beginning with "claim 1", with each following claim numbered in order. This is why it is critical that you spend as much time as needed, but not any more time or effort, since you do want to be first to file, to understand as many variations of your invention as can be contrived.

Changing the conversation: When the time comes to draft claim sets that engender the proper scope for your objective monopoly rights, you will be at the point of changing over from a layman's claim representation to the legal, finally reviewed formal claims for your invention. This is a big step, but if you hand over your invention definition to patent counsel too early, they likely can get trigger-happy, drafting legal claims before you have reduced your P-E to its simplest form using the best grammar (vocabulary terms with their meaning, in your glossary).

If you pass the marshmallow test and employ counsel at the right time to finally edit and provide a set of proposed formal claims, they will most likely be constructed in a way that you will understand and that will meet your criteria for being broad enough in scope to capture the derivative variations of your invention without overstepping the boundaries by being too broad. Any claim made by the smartest guys in the room, which may unknowingly include you, that are too broad, may prove to be unpatentable over the prior art used during prosecution or force defense against irrelevant embodiments.

When your drafted application publishes, the nature of your patentability will turn on how the claims at the end of the patent application include sufficient distinguishing characteristics of your P-E to be seen as directed to a new and unobvious invention, in relationship to all relevant prior art that was known and considered during prosecution. If the examiner finds that the claims of the patent application, as compared with any relevant prior art, are too broad so as to be unpatentable over that art, then the applicant will be told by reply, during prosecution, you will have an opportunity to limit the claims, narrowing the scope in meaningful and useful ways to refocus the claimed invention in order to distinguish it from the applied prior art. As stated, in the end, the published claims in your issued application will be used to judge whether your granted patent has what I call functional validity. Will it ensure your monopoly against anyone practicing your invention, or will it ensure you have freedom to operate with your invention if accused by another that you are practicing theirs? When this analysis is done, the assessment will be based on how at least one claim reads on the offending object. In the ADVANCED-PRACTITIONER level, I share a method that ensures you are going into the fray with your best grammar in your filed claims.

Changing the conversation: I want to return to the issue of preparing an invention disclosure and giving it to your patent counsel as soon as you can. The IP SAVVYS approach supports engagement with counsel on converting your invention into a patent application when it is the right time. The key to changing this conversation is how you think about your invention in the context of your product development life cycle. When you are working on your invention, turning it into the P-E, as the product version you will introduce in the progression of building your market over the life of the product line, it will have multidimensional ways of being represented and described at each stage. It's just like the developmental life of a child, moving through the stages from adolescent to adult. Focus on the P-E first, and don't worry about how it will finally look in a patent application, because with the IP SAVVY approach, your IDPAW holds the Schwartz Patent Rubric at its core. For this reason, as you prepare each version of your IDPAW, you will be getting closer to a representation that can be translated into a patent application. The IDPAW has you drafting without even knowing it!

What are you doing in the IDPAW that changes the conversation? With the Schwartz Method, each passing week or month, as you noodle your P-E, you will be asking yourself a dozen or more questions, and the answers to the questions will change, until they stop changing. When they stop changing, you are ready to have your conversation about translating your invention into a patent application. As an IP SAVVY, you do this as part of continuous improvement during product development. Know that by documenting some of these details in your IDPAW for each P-E, you are on your way to providing the core representation of what the drafting exercise is designed to express for the patent office.

This is how to think about it: in product development, you are continually defining the problem you are solving with your invention's P-E. When you can articulate the way in which what you have is different, you are winning. You will also identify how the key aspects of the P-E that make it different work together to produce your unexpected result. You will be explaining the form and function of the operation of the P-E.

Does it stand alone? If it does, how does it replace what existed before? If it's part of another thing, how does it fit in? Does it replace something or improve that other thing and if so, how? Are any of the unique functional elements you have articulated found in any other product? What are the commercial market benefits of this version of the P-E and to whom? Is what you are offering a nice-to-have or a must-have (can't live without it)?

Think of the game of secrets where you tell a first person the secret and they tell the next person and so forth. At the end, will the articulation of the secret be the same? If it is, you are winning. Another test is to make believe you are telling Abe Lincoln, someone who is smart and capable but who knows nothing about your technology. Also try thinking of the target for this explanation as a fifth grader. If they get it, then you're winning.

5.4 Further steps in perfecting the P-E

You will be making iterative entries into your IDPAW as an integral part of your product development phases. Here is a further breakdown of the fundamental questions you will be answering as you create each feasible representation of your P-E in its best mode:

Depict each part or step of your current version. Identify what each element contributes to the significance of your inventive step and the unexpected behavior of this version.

How would you make it? Describe how you would combine the minimal set of elements into it in such a way that someone else could read, acknowledge it as understood, and practice it. Be sure to identify and explain to yourself all of the things that can be removed without breaking it. Make believe that other person is you until you have convinced yourself it's clear, then ask another person in a confidential collaboration. Be sure to include any and all relevant parameters, ranges, ways of making alternatives, and unessential but marketable optional features that could be part of a release downstream.

For each part of this embodiment that is completely new, explain how that part is related to previous stuff. If there is other stuff, note how what you have done has been modified to make it work in your invention. If you are using preexisting stuff in your innovation with parts or steps of prior stuff that have not changed, explain how your invention is using them in new ways.

Is there a sequence for the workings of your P-E?

If the notion of sequence is meaningful, then how do you start using it, how do you keep using it, and how do you stop using it?

When it's used in each phase, how do the pieces interoperate or the steps flow, in what order, and what is changed as a result of that use or step?

In the formulation of this version of the P-E, note which part or step would completely disable your invention if removed or changed. When you can't take away any part, you can stop for now.

This would be the time to complete your IDPAW entry with specific figures, along with labels and item names (don't worry about reference numbers yet). Identify everything.

As a penultimate step in completing your IDPAW entry, write an English sentence with the terms that describes how the parts are connected (the layman's claim).

As a last step, make a detailed summary of any alternative way to implement a lesser version of your product or method that doesn't use your stuff, and describe how it works and why.

Now, before archiving your last iteration of the IDPAW, answer these additional derivative versions of the differentiation questions:

Once you have done your best, iterative reduction to practice, what is the next best change in your parts or steps that can produce an equivalent result?

Is there any way that components or steps could be joined into a simpler representation, essentially eliminating some part of your claimed embodiment?

Do any of these alterations improve the operation and/or reduce its cost?

Do any of these changes suggest different utility or intended application?

How do any of these changes target the technology classification for your proposed P-E? Being mindful about widening or refocusing your classification during this stage will allow you to focus your iterative searches.

Always go back to the drawing board with your layman's claim and rework your best mode if there is a way to construct your inventive matter with any new insights. After reworking the components into the simplest form known to you now, have you found the single best words that can be used to identify each part in your description that can unambiguously be used to state your inventive behavior and define your claim's scope?

Always keep an eye open for new applications as well as ones that will not perform as well. While working with your own inventive matter, try to be mindful of "accidents" in using the elements and what the result of that unexpected event yielded. Often your intuition is taking you into a nuance that your logical brain might not have inferred. Go with accidents as they are the key to best mode, reduction to practice. These insights will contribute to your discussion in the background of the invention after you have quiesced your layman's claim. The ability to explain your invention to the examiner is substantially enhanced by seeing the upsides and downsides of your P-E.

In some instances, your invention may operate only within certain parameters. These must be captured and included if they are integral to your best mode of operation. These can take the form of dimensions, weights, temperatures, materials, pressures, or ratios of any of these.

Does your invention include any unique materials that must be used alone or in combination for your best mode?

As with the other properties of your invention, keeping these as trade secrets is as important as any other processes in your IP workflow. At some point on this pathway, your description will be depicted by turning the labeled parts and terms from your glossary into formal figures with reference numbers that tie back into the figures and your description of each of the parts. This will become the part of the detailed description covering your formal claim.

5.5 Moving your invention into a form that can be adequately represented before deciding on what type of patent application to file

Since the only thing that matters in the end are your claims, your internal drafting is now completely integrated with your product development life cycle. Each time you write your English sentence (what I called your layman's claim), you will be following my ABC rule: Always Be Claiming. This ABC rule is your key to changing the IP conversation at each stage of your effort to move into a commercially viable embodiment. It's not that different than the ABC rule from Glenn Gary Glenn Ross, a classic Alec Baldwin pep talk on making a deal and closing a sale. Here you continually trial close on your own understanding of your invention with the goal of generating the next best version of a pure layman's claim. Trust me, given that piece of my UPL, any competent attorney, or at some point, even yourself, can convert that sentence into a formal legal claim at next to no cost. You should always write this claim before any real patent drafting by an outside counsel is authorized. When you use this part of my UPL and follow this Schwartz Method guiding principle, you will assuredly not spend precious utility patent budget dollars on the wrong thin, and you will benefit immensely during prosecution.

In order to constantly quality yourself in this iterative effort, you will need to keep asking yourself these questions and remain as honest with yourself as humanly possible. When you have quiesced the answers, you may be ready to turn your layman's claim over to a professional for legal formalization in a finally drafted patent application.

5.6 Layman vs. legal claim representations

As a further summary, and as you will learn in IP-BC, I advocate for what I call the layman's claim as a critical entry into your first IDPAW. Once this sentence is stable, then and only then do you work out the legal claim form. When you advance through the IP-BC levels, you will become even more focused on your P-E. It is the object of your invention that represents the simplest and best mode of conveying your novel, inventive utility, and its unexpected behavior. That representation can be delivered in two ways. The first way is the simplest and easiest to understand, and it is what I have explained as the layman's representation (in the form of an English, non-legalese run-on sentence). The second way is in a legal/formal claim.

In IP-BC and the Schwartz Method, these two forms are equivalent (they cover one and the same thing), with their sole difference being the legal claiming variations used to ensure a properly scoped monopoly.

Changing the conversation: This sounds simple, and it really is. You will find a template for the iterative grammar of a layman's claim in the appendix as well as in my course. It has a very definite structure, and it is comprised of a set of elements that not only tie together in the run-on sentence, but also tie directly back into the Schwartz Patent Rubric in the IDPAW and the creation sequence of each of the sections. This is probably a good time to review the appendix with where I reveal the inner workings of TSM.

The structure of an English-language claim can be made using your P-E figure (and what should be your figure 1) and your glossary of terms that identify the critical elements for your inventive step. In the Schwartz Method, the template is initially developed into an ID-PAW entry, which includes your latest version of the claim template

(Section 6). When that IDPAW version is extracted as a document, it includes all of the critical descriptive matter you might have been asked to provide to patent counsel in their invention disclosure form, with the fundamental difference that it now is structured in a form that not only integrates the claim into a functional target document, but it will have all of the necessary and sufficient content to allow it to be transformed into a Schwartz Method UCPA. The guidance here is to press on with the framework taught in IP-BC/the Schwartz Method as the answer to providing an invention disclosure document. You may hear that I use different language and definitions for utility patenting drafting and construction, and that is actually the case. As you can now agree, my rubrics "UPL grammar", in the form of the IDPAW, not only conforms to MPEP, but it is a more formal version of what you are typically asked for as the invention disclosure. By breaking the patent formalism down and reverse engineering it, our templates (and their names) form an engineering form of the typical invention disclosure document, and at the end of the day, that is the magic of the Schwartz Method. See a claim form following. This might be a good time to revisit the appendix and the glossary where TSM is detailed the UPL and GP are explained. To scale your IP SAVVY capabilities, use the coupon for ADVANCED or upgrade and use IDPAW as a dynamic document in the IP-BC/ ADVANCED-PRACTITIONER level (https://www.ipboostcamp.com).

Claim Drafting Worksheet Section C (Section 6)

A (B1 *(name of the inventive embodiment in this claim)*

x
_____

for B4 *(why:explain to the examiner what the inventive claim is to do)*

x
_____

comprising D'
(list each element of the claimed embodiment with exact terms-NUMBER EACH TERM BY NAME)
      (a)
      (b)
      (c)
and where(a,b,c...) further comprises D
(list each sub-element if it is needed for the claim to "work"-NUMBER EACH TERM BY SUB-NAME)
      (a)
      (b)
      (c)
and further when D"
    ___(a,b,c & any related subparts) are ex. Instantiated, how connected, interoperate__
    _____(((*describe how the parts interrelate in the preferred embodiment*)))_____

x
_____

such that D'''
    ____(((*describe the nature of the transformation that occurs*)))_____
    ____(((*and the unexpected thing/event happens when the embodiment is operated*)))___

x
_____

and as a result the TRANSFORMATION THAT OCCURS B4 / B3
    _____(((*explain outcome that is the surprise of the interaction of the elements*)))____
    _____(((*and how it overcomes the prior limitations*)))_____

x
_____

iQ

Fig.12 TSM's Section C claim template (Section 6 of a formal patent)

You may hear that there are subtle layers in the nuance of formal claim language and terminology, as used for legal claiming. For example, you will be told the use of the term *having means* when establishing functionality is preferred, and using the words *at least one or more, comprising substantially, consisting of, including one or more, a plurality,* and so forth are best practice terms that you won't be able to understand or master. In other words, you cannot develop the claim structure for your invention, and you must leave it to a professional. You will hear that the winding precedence of case law from federal circuit courts and the US Supreme Court, as well as the rereleases of MPEP guidelines, makes claiming an art known only to IP shamans. Further, as much as the patent office seeks uniform interpretation in the art groups, examiners with different training and with clever supervisors from their art group can unintentionally impose different interpretations of claims, not only because of differences in skill, but also because of limitations in their understanding of your inventive matter. The notion of complexity in claiming will be clouded, and you may be told that it is extremely complicated to construct good-quality patent claims with the right scope to properly protect your invention.

In fact, if you use the IDPAW to capture the fundamental idea of your FOG , the flash of genius in the ah-ha moment when the true inventor becomes fully aware of his or her discovery, the form and function of the object of your invention that conveys the delightfully unexpected behavior of your invention, the unique manner in which your form uses a minimalist set of elements for its construction, comprising what is otherwise your novelty of your inventive step (elimination of something in the prior art that was cumbersome, unnecessary, expensive or that otherwise made the prior stuff hideous), you will be able to set forth a layman's claim in your series of IDPAW iterations.

Your set of progressively smarter layman's claims of your invention, turned into the UCD, will evolve conterminously and continuously during product development with your P-E, to establish the best internal core of your patent application. When you do this, you have changed the conversation because what you have developed (you are drafting the whole time!) is a sufficiently well-defined structure designed to ensure a viable patent application can be generated from it. When you do it this way, you will get a patent application that you will not only understand, but whose scope you will be able to sort out and control as you integrate and interpret how all of the prior art applied during the fray, along your pathway to patentship.

5.7 Fundamental difference between the structure of a patent application and the Schwartz Patent Rubric

Changing the conversation: More about offering as much descriptive material as counsel asks for in a functional template they refer to as an invention disclosure. In fact, the UCD formalism does the trick. It will ensure you constructively develop the essential elements that will become your patent draft. Quiesce your P-E using my iterative method for patent application drafting, and you will win at the budget bottom line as well as on the commercial stage.

When you use the Schwartz Method, you will be guided through the steps in which you develop a succinct simplification of what will eventually be in the first figure and the first claim of your invention, when filed as a patent application.

One key point to make about language and terms for parts of your invention, along with numbers for the elements themselves, is that you can make up your own names for components in your P-E, use them in a glossary, define them in your detailed description, and eventually number them in the drawings and detailed description of the invention, this is all done downstream, in the final drafting.

The trick is not to allow anyone to start a bible patent draft prematurely, but rather to craft the documents from the inside-out using the Schwartz Method. You will see how this works and appreciate the wisdom of my pathway to patentship. What I share in the following section is an outline of the MPEP framework of a patent application when it is translated from a UCD to a UCPA, finally using the "typical scripted language" that is embedded into an actual, finally filed patent application. If you do proceed, it will look like this in the filing packet.

5.8 What it's going to look like in the end – the patent application formation

This section provides the MPEP section format and uses the contextual language that is typically part of the formal patent application. I provide some drafting hints as well. The section numbering is based on rule 113, and will incorporate translated contents from the TSM IDPAW template, the UCD, and the UCPA.

Remember that the order of delivery (in the actual filing) is not the order of creation. Using the Schwartz Method and the Schwartz Patent Rubric, you will use this fundamental GP in the most efficient way to construct an airtight utility patent that is right the first time and de-risked from FOARs. That is how you are going to change your IP conversation about drafting the best mode specification and claims on your invention. This section is not a how-to on drafting. Here is the format of a final patent application:

TITLE

When you finally choose your title—something you will keep reworking as you follow the iterative sequence in drafting—you will finally choose words for your title that are based on your finally drafted first claim, but that will be even higher (as in one level more generic), with simple, descriptive language that does not rely on any special language you might choose or use in your marketing verbiage.

SECTION 1: ABSTRACT (OF THE DISCLOSURE)

Using about 150 words (think a TWEET of your invention)

"Object Y is provided … "

This paragraph provides a simple description of the operation of the claim representing the P-E. Therefore, it is essential that the inventive feature of the innovation be known and clearly articulated, and that the graphic representation of that embodiment be carefully selected for the first figure of the application, and that the general language here depicts that in layman's terms.

The abstract of the invention is filed in the DOC PAK on the last page, but if the application is allowed and publishes, it is placed as the first page of the published patent.

SECTION 2: BACKGROUND OF THE INVENTION

"This invention relates to … "

First state the standard objects in the field of the invention by either quoting the descriptive matter from the classification guide or using descriptive matter from relevant prior art in the field and subfield of this specific invention. This is the space into which the invention is being introduced. State these elements as TYPE A, TYPE B, TYPE C. Then discuss current prior art and known public solutions stating the limitations of those known solutions in the form of PROBLEM A, PROBLEM B, and PROBLEM C. Then specifically state what is new in this invention by listing its new aspects such as NEW ASPECT A, NEW ASPECT B, and NEW ASPECT C.

SECTION 3: SUMMARY

The summary offers a non-legalese restatement of each of the claims and is like an introduction to the monopoly rights you are seeking. It makes your patent easy to read (remember, claims can use special language to define scope, and that may make reading them difficult at first). The summary is always created as the last step in preparing a patent application since the claims must quiesce before it is written. It should copy the exact terms used in your claims while conveying each claim in simple language.

SECTION 4: Brief Description of the Drawings/and ALL Figures

This section identifies each figure with its figure number and includes a one-sentence description of what is depicted. Figure 1 should always be your best effort to convey what is in the first independent claim in your claims section. It is one of the checks and balances the examiner uses to see if you have focused on your P-E. A tell-tale indication that a patent is a bible patent is when Figure 1 shows an amorphous representation of the invention in the world in which the invention is being placed.

The actual figures/drawings follow the brief description in the Schwartz Method formalism. Each figure depicts core structural features that represent your novelty and how the pieces fit together. Some depictions will use flowcharts. Figures must be prepared in line with drawing requirements. I do not go into non-provisional formatting details here. You can provide hand-drawn figures in a provisional application, but when you are submitting a non-provisional application, you must follow the exact drawing requirements (well documented—easy to find and follow). Generally, you should keep to simple black-and-white line drawings and although no shading is normal, you can use dots or hash lines if they enable clarity. If you must have color, you have to petition to do so.

SECTION 5: Detailed Description

This is always the largest section of the patent application because it provides a complete and thorough description that supports the claims for the invention. After the claims have quiesced, it is possible to cut and paste all of the claims here, then edit in connecting language and a better explanation of the inventive steps and the unexpected behavior of your first claim, in order to ensure the examiner knows that you know what you invented. The level of detail required is sufficient so that anyone skilled in the art can make and use your invention. This section basically explains the core claims, conveying in readily understood language how your invention works. Your detailed description should focus on how the claimed elements interoperate to provide your unexpected, delightful inventive behavior If you developed a solid glossary as recommended in the Schwartz Method, then the terms used, and their reference numbers will always align with each of the parts of the invention as depicted in the figures. In providing support for the claims, again, it cannot be overstated that it is here that all reference numbers for each of the elements of the invention detailed in the figures are identified and explained, using the same names (terms) and the same reference numbers. This is why a glossary is a must. If you leave out a numbered item or fail to use it correctly and consistently, you will be in technical default and you will get a rule 111 and 112 rejection. These rejections can be fatal if you don't have support for a correction or if you failed to draw out the details in alignment with the claims. This is why copying the final claims here is a way to ensure you don't fall into any traps that will result in a messy file wrapper you have to fix after filing.

SECTION 6: Claims

The claims section is framed as the last section. It consists of one or more numbered claims, beginning with #1 and incrementing by one for each additional claim (independent or dependent—a dependent claim references the independent claim immediately preceding it). The patent claims are what matters most since they unequivocally state the monopoly rights you are seeking as the inventor. They specify what you want to prevent others from making, using, or selling if and when your patent is granted.

Changing the conversation: You may be told that these run-on sentences will give your grammar teacher an angina, because they are the most difficult to read and understand. Why? In order to establish scope, they will also employ special words with special meaning. If you realize that the writing is intentionally a run-on sentence, then they're actually easy to read. If you understand the specification and the definition of the terms and their intent (proper antecedent reference for the P-E inventive step and unexpected behavior), then they are easy to understand because patent law requires that the first claim, written as a single sentence, is the broadest scope for the intended monopoly. If you don't understand your legal claim, then don't approve or file it yet. If the claim was crafted by legal counsel from your UCD, then there should be no overreaching and no misunderstanding of what you are asking for from the patent office when you file.

5.9 More on actual drafting guidelines: Moving through a set of IDPAW drafts

In my DIAAY approach, there is a point to "cut bait or fish." This is the point when you turn over your last IDPAW into a UCD. Next you translate your UCD into a UCPA. This is an actual patent application draft, and it has the claim for your P-E, even though the first version of that document might still just have terms naming parts in figures without any numbers.

All of the bits about including descriptions of the egregious limitations of the alternatives, as you would craft in the Schwartz Method Section B, Background (one of the very last steps in the Schwartz Method), and specific implementation details of the alternative ways, will ensure the examiner knows that you understand what your invention is and what its scope is.

When the detailed description of the actual patent application is drafted, the terms in your figures will be converted to a set of unique reference numbers that align with each of the drawings in the figures section. At the same time, you will be copying and pasting your claims into the detail description section, using the grammar of the claim as the bones of your description. Then you will draft a series of paragraphs, likely one for each claim, into English sentences and use the reference numbers that have been finally assigned. I also recommend placing the critical numbers in the claims next to each identical term you reference. When this part of drafting is done, you are at a full patent application core and the other sections can be completed by anyone who read and understood your invention. At this point, every number is unique, every term is tied to a unique number, and used consistently/exactly/identically everywhere from

Section 1 to Section 6 (refer to the aforementioned formal patent format).

Changing the conversation: You may be told that the process of drafting a well-constructed patent application is time-consuming and expensive. If you followed the Schwartz Method procedures for the IDPAW, then you should pat yourself on the back for not taking any shortcuts. And much like Shakespeare writing *A Mid-Summer Nights Dream* in one weekend, after thinking about it for ten years, by integrating the IDPAW into your product development life cycle (hopefully in a lot less time than ten years), the drafting of the final patent application will be quick, clear, and cost-effective and is more a process of translation than creation.

Changing the conversation: If you take any shortcuts, like filing a provisional application with no claim, with the goal of getting your priority date in the first-to-file system, you will be in for a rude awakening. This filing will likely prove to be useless, providing little or no protection. Any patent application only protects what is claimed and supported directly in the detailed description of the invention. You may be told that it's important to not get caught up in the details of documenting your invention when asked for an invention disclosure document. The last thing you want to do is pass the baton to patent counsel with a general inventive description. You must get into the iterative description of your invention using the IDPAW template and notebook entries, since this is the only way you will be able to generate a utility patent application with a claim at the end of your product development life cycle.

Globally, we are all now harmonized in a first-to-file convention treaty, so everyone is in a race to be first to file at their patent office. The earliest filing date for what you want claimed is the winner. If you want to draft a non-provisional compliant patent application, whether you file it as a provisional or not (see next section), your goal must be to get the draft right the first time, with a claim scoped to your intended monopoly. Even if you file a provisional application with a layman's claim, if you flip it to a non-provisional application at the end of the one year provided, you can rewrite the claim in formal claim language (with all of the key nuances in that grammar), as long as you don't add any new matter or change any terms in the antecedent reference. The implication of this for changing the conversation is that if you really know the Schwartz patent rubric and how to ensure the core invention is specified and claimed, you can keep your priority date, formalize the claim, and flip it , providing you don't try to expand the scope of the filed claim, without having a supporting detailed description from the original application filing. I cover more of this in the section on patent strategy and tactics.

If you're told that it's more important to get the invention disclosure document done quickly so you don't lose the race to the patent office, think twice. If you are unorganized and have a poor or ineffective patent capture process, you don't really have a choice and you will be forced to rush what may prove to be a weakly specified description to the patent altar. If you use the iterative Schwartz Method, with progressively refined IDPAW drafts, then you can and will change the conversation about what is filed and when, not to mention how it is prosecuted.

Just be wary when asked to provide an invention disclosure document early because the steps in converting that to a patent, filing it, and prosecuting it could unintentionally and unavoidably turn into a black hole that sucks in all of your patent spending and more.

When you develop the progressive IDPAW entries, you will be providing enough detail to enable it's translation into a high-quality patent application that has real SCA. As you will see during prosecution, if you can keep the file wrapper clean, you will have a stronger patent issue. More on that later.

In detailing the IDPAW and how you create one (see the AD-VANCED or ADVANCED-PRACTITIONER IP-BC levels), you will always be claiming and augmenting your iterative representation with the critical details for preparing and filing a complete DOC PAK. You may be told that invention disclosure is the key to allowing an experienced patent professional to proceed because they are the shamans and the only ones who know what to include and how to include it. That is simply not true. At the end of the day, when you know the rubric of what to include and how to include it, you will self-manage your way to the point in a conversation with IP counsel in which you control that complete dialogue, ask the questions about scope based on finally drafted claims, and factor in the elements of any complementary inventive material to build a portfolio without getting trapped into dividing a bible patent that inadequately covers either of your real P-Es.

Don't rest comfortably on the delivery of any general description, as if you're on your pathway to patentship. The tough work is in iterating on the P-E, the language to describe it, and the layman's claim for that version of it. If you give that task to counsel too early, you're in for a roller coaster ride where you go around and around on finally defining the P-E, all the while, getting more inscrutable fees on each loop.

When you do hire a patent professional to draft your patent application (if you are not at the point of doing that totally on your own), then they will do the translation from the IDPAW into a UCD and then into a UCPA (covered in detail in the 30-day IP-BC IP challenge using your own inventive matter). This is the essence of my UPL and GP. That grammar and semantics not only directs your

IDPAW lab notebook entries, but it also guides the way to ask counsel to help you in the IP hunt. That is the end game in changing the conversation.

Do it almost all yourself, and you will have a good DIAAY. You will save more than 70 percent of your drafting and prosecution costs once you are into it. The steps are completely intertwined in a lock-step sequence that is unbreakable. When you begin with a vision of the scope of your claims in mind, you will end up where you choose to be and want to be at the end of what will still be a grueling process.

As you move through the drafting steps, you will always be claiming and in so doing, you will be able to sort out how to fill the discontinuity you have identified with your inventive matter. Can you do it with just one invention/patent application, or will you be able to create a portfolio with related filings that represent a product line, or a way to engage and develop the market by offering an array of new problem-solving products? I discuss this further in the section on patent strategy, as your business goals and models will determine how you approach the drafting and filing plan over time. If you're licensing or developing a product line, things will be considerably different. If you're going it alone or partnering with others, the game will change considerably. You may start out one way, then realize you have opened Pandora's box (positive connotation) and change your IP and business strategy. Again, you won't know what to do until you're doing it, and that's nothing to fear. As with anything, the more you do almost all yourself, the less likely you will be to step in the potholes along the pathway to patentship.

Remember that your patent application can have only one invention in it, so be careful if you know more about what else you want to patent at the time of filing. If you can sequence what you know, and it makes sense in terms of your product line and business model, then don't try to include all of it in your first filing. If your inventive matter can go in multiple directions, you could include it all and divide your patents later, but the terminal disclaimer date clock will have started at the time of your first filing. If your other elements should have been patented on their own, you will be required to divide them out along with having to file terminal disclaimers on the claim sets, which will shorten the clock (basically twenty years minus the next date of separation) for each of their monopolies. journey because the steps are so intimately interwoven.

Your goal with each IDPAW entry will be to pull together focused explanations of everything about your patentable matter, from this layman's sentence to the critical terms and keywords that define your classification field. Along the way, you will use the IDPAW template to iteratively expand the properties of your winning preparation effort. You will iteratively focus on the capture any of the egregious limitations of the competing inventions for that iteration of your P-E. Remember that you might find that you thought you knew your invention, but then realized it was something else. That could change how your IDPAW tree propagates and what you capture along with it. You don't have to have everything ready at once, which is the downfall of trying to give counsel an invention disclosure too early. With the Schwartz Method, you will come out of the FOG (see my blog post on this), as the Schwartz Method elicits the incremental details about your invention as you become truly mindful of them.

When you get closer to preparing your filing documents, which will include your UCD as a UCPA translated patent target document, you can refine how you reference your key prior art, by pointing out the parts that you invent over and why they don't teach your invention. It is important to keep things on an even keel and to be honest and positive in identifying your patentable insights. You will be saving these up during preparation and incorporating them into the information disclosure document (IDS) explanation. Remember that your statements and their tone will reflect back into your file wrapper during prosecution and that your words may be weaponized against you. The IDS may in some circles be as critical as the patent application itself. Remember, every cohort has different goals and objectives, so if someone is writing your IDS for you, you will want to monitor that and ensure it's consistent with your objectives during prosecution. You will see that in the DIAAY model, you will be engaged in managing your prosecution steps, and your words will come back around to be a part of the dialogue that ensues.

As you work through these steps capturing inventive content on the pathway, each of your insights about the limitations of your prior art findings can lead you to a new definition of the problem you're solving and even to an array of new ways to solve the same or a related problem. For this reason, I hold firm to the conviction that you should not be forced to search too soon in the same sense of why you should not fill out invention disclosure documents too early. If you look at what the others have done before you know what you have, you might not stumble onto your true P-E. The layman's drafting process using the Schwartz Method is designed to ferret all of this out ,while optimizing your P-E discoveries and representations.

In developing each iteration of your P-E IDPAW entry, you will be thinking about how cool your invention is, (the single metaphor that makes it memorable and a must have for the user of your product). In each iteration, you are working to reduce to practice your visual representation in its simplest form, with names for all of its parts. Some things are process centric, like software, so in that case, you will be using other graphic techniques to share your method. Flowcharts have many graphic options that allow for the visual depiction of every kind of process behavior, so you should pick the graphical tool that is suitable to your technology area. One very powerful tool that is of potential value for software is the structured analysis design technique, which has a drawing form for the process and an interwoven drawing form for the data. This technique has been around for decades, and when its core principles are understood, it will be a powerful tool for specifying software. That is only one example. As the expert, your selection of representation tools is very important.

The figures will eventually have to follow the MPEP prescription, so you should familiarize yourself with it. In the IDPAW, keep to simple line drawings when you can and try not to use shading or color. Be sure to name every part (remember that numbers are not needed yet. Always make a glossary at the same time). Account for each named part in your layman's claim for this P-E. When the P-Es converge and you are ready to flip the IDPAW into a UCD, you will apply numbers to each element, and they will be in your more robust claim. Not until you get to a UCPA will you worry about the way the claim is written, so don't overthink all of that yet. When the detailed description is finally written, based on a completely quiesces layman's claim, it will support every element named in the claim.

Changing the conversation: You may be told that the claims are the most complicated and take the most skill, so they should only be done by a patent agent or patent attorney. Yes, in the UCPA, the first pass is made at claims written in legal terms, and you may need help. So don't get freaked out early about this as the reason for turning over an invention disclosure. If you have a set of IDPAW entries that have coalesced in a clear notion of what you want to patent, then the time will come to lawyer up and legalize the claims.

It will always be clear which figures you need to write the layman's claim, so if you are told that you will have difficulty with this, that is very far from the truth because only you really know which ones they really are. In this step, you are re-focusing the known part of what will eventually be in your formal patent submission. The key to the Schwartz patent rubric is iterating on which figure is key, identifying what should ultimately be Figure 1 in your submission, and supporting independent Claim 1 in the detailed description of your filing. Even though you are not drafting the claims now, you are providing figures that show the workings of your invention. When you are at the point of converting the IDPAW to the UCD and the UCPA, you are supporting enablement. The figures you show must work and be expressed or represented in your classification technology space. When the actual drafting proceeds, it is more or less just a translation (subject to my comment on legal claiming). You will need to make sure each of the references from the figures, to the claims, to the detailed description all tie together. That is called antecedent reference. When you audit your patent draft before filing, that is called de-risking for fatal office action rejections, the rule 111,112,113 FOAR errors.

It's one thing to get bounced for failings on patent eligibility, novelty, and nonobviousness (rules 100, 101, and 102), but it's egregious if you get bounced on lacking enablement and its mate, unambiguous antecedent reference. These rejections for rules 111, 112, and 113 can and will kill you. They should never happen. With the Schwartz Method, they will never happen on your watch, and that is the ultimate conversation game changer.

The basics are easy to understand since the figures show utility and tie everything together. If a figure is described in a claim, then its description will be articulated in the translation step. Remember, each term should have a line pointing to a part of the figure. That's good enough for now. If you turn over your stuff too soon, and your patent counsel applies the numbers to a P-E that must be changed, it's going to be an expensive do-over.

Eventually, when you do get to the detailed description of the invention, if you waited long enough, having a good DIAAY, then it will be possible to take the first set of related claims (i.e., a claim set comprised of the independent claim and dependent claims for the unexpected behavior of the P-E), you can just cut and paste them into the section titled "Detailed Description," and rework them to state what is between the lines (remember the claim is designed to establish scope so it will be illusive), and make sure that the description ensures the most critical reader of your patent application, the examiner, will get how it works. Here is where definite and unambiguous explanations are required so that someone else can follow your train of thought and duplicate what you say you invented. I know I'm repeating myself, but this is one of the most fundamental guiding principles of the Schwartz Method, which is to unequivocally tell it like it is and claim it like it is. Anyone putting a bible patent into play for you that tries to obfuscate what you are claiming will get you to hell in a handbasket. There is no way any draft like that will ever fly. If during prosecution (see later), such a mess of a patent application is finessed into an allowance, it will be weak with every flaw exposed in its file wrapper for all to see, especially your investors and your competitors.

So, when you do ultimately provide a finished explanation of your invention, with enough detail that anyone skilled in the classification art can make and use your invention, you've completed the translation. Take a deep breath, and then take another look. Have you done the interweave in accordance with the Schwartz Method guiding principles for unambiguity, antecedent reference, and full enablement for the P-E. Did you really provide the best known mode of operation known to you at this time? Does the draft filing and the claims truly read on your invention, and have you read and understood it? If you're told not to worry—that it's all there but it's in legalese so you can't really understand its final form—beware. If you toss something like that over the transom at the patent office, you will surely have a horrible experience during prosecution, and it will be expensive and could cost you your filing with an abandonment. When you use the Schwartz Method, you will improve your chances.

6.0. Fundamentals of changing the filing conversation: Types of filing (PE, AE, PPH, SP)

6.1 Basics of changing the prosecution pathway

When you look at the MPEP on how to choose a filing method, there will be a morass of legalese, and it is easy to get confused. If you decide to use one of the methods designed to move prosecution along, you can readily get the forms and fees to accomplish your objectives. For now, I give you some basic insights into the options and why you might want to use one or the other. As you would expect, normal examination (NE) requests can be made using the standard filing forms and fee submission papers. Here are more details about the additional pathways to prosecution, how they work, and why you might want to use them.

6.2 Accelerated examination (AE)

As explained earlier, the goal of this program is for applicants to obtain a final disposition within twelve months of filing the initial application. The reason to use this is really twofold. Not only do you want to get a final disposition in a predetermined interval (less than one year), but you are also given the opportunity to halo the examination by making very detailed arguments on your patentability. What this means is rather than trust the examiner, you do all the hard work first.

Changing the conversation: You may be told that to do this you will have to pay a lot more in legal preparation fees for the search and analysis. To use this procedure, your drafting tactics will need to anticipate that you are going to do this, so you don't have to pay excessive patent counsel fees to "back fit" your filing documents. Do this in line with your UCD conversion to the UCPA, and you will be way ahead of the game. It will take more work, but it won't actually cost you a lot more money. It will just be more tedious and harder to get a compliant pre-search document set.

Changing the conversation: Since you will have to go on record and characterize the scope of your claims, you may be told that this is something you don't want to do because it could limit the scope of the claims in the granted patent if a patent infringement case occurs later. This occurs as a result of something called file wrapper estoppel – which stipulates that you cannot later argue an interpretation of your claims that is different from what you argued during prosecution of the application. That said, if you know the scope you want, and you don't want to invite infringers with claim scope was too broad, then you should be mindful in arguing the scope as part of your filing, and not afraid to do that.

The AE program provides applicants one month to reply to an office action. The penalty for failing to meet this time frame is that the application goes abandoned. Applicants have the option of filing a continuing application to prevent the subject matter from becoming abandoned.

Changing the conversation: You may be told that the time and expense of an AE program, the risk of file wrapper estopple, and the risk of abandonment if you can't respond to an office action within one month should give you pause and steer you away from the AE option. In reality, if you want the best bite of the apple in the first office action, you should prepare for this during the UCD-to-UCPA conversion so that you can file this way if it serves your business goals. Would you rather know the truth and nothing but the truth early rather than end up in a protracted prosecution and find out later that you missed critical prior art and have to abandon the application after paying lots of fees to patent counsel?

6.3 Prioritized examination (PE)

If you need to move your ideas quickly, this will also allow you to get a final disposition within about twelve months. You can get this special status with fewer requirements than the AE program, especially without having to prepare a detailed pre-examination search report. Compared to AE, this is easier to file and get your determination. As with AE, the decision to seek a formal determination on patentability in one year may play into similar business goals. It can assist with getting investment funds or tie in with a planned product announcement. If there is a question about whether your product can be protected and whether you could exercise your freedom to operate without risking intentional infringement, the final office position can be beneficial. Prioritized examination is available for a fee at the time of filing an original utility patent application or as part of a request for continuing prosecution with an RCE for a utility patent application. You might choose to use this procedure and have the patent office do most of your hard work to reduce the risk of having to litigate an issued patent. If your application is pending and a competitor enters the market, this procedure is akin to the old interference process—getting an answer from the patent office against a would-be infringer and getting into a better position to send a cease and desist letter. Since the first-to-file issue will rear its head, if a competitor's product that reads on your application says, "patent pending," then this will be a way to promptly establish your filing date so you can decide whether to take action. Forearmed is forewarned, and a way to stave off expensive downstream litigation risks.

6.4 Patent Prosecution Highway (PPH)

The Patent Prosecution Highway (PPH) does not yield a final disposition within any predefined. Prosecution will proceed under normal rules, but if an examiner in one office (ex. EPO) has made a favorable ruling on your claims, you can request your examiner use that ruling as a jumping-off point for the prosecution in your home country. If you filed conterminously in the United States at the same time as filing with the EPO , it may prove that the international search PCT process could produce a result sooner. The EPO countries included in the PPH option are most countries in Europe, along with Australia, Canada, China, Japan, South Korea. Submit a claim granted by another patent office that participates in the PPH program along with the favorable international search report indicating that at least one claim has novelty, inventive step, and industrial applicability, and you can get a faster first office action from a US examiner. Again, since international search reports are typically made before a patent claim is granted by the US Patent Office, you can use this procedure to enter the PPH program and get a faster determination. You can also use the PPH program to expedite prosecution in other countries following allowance in the United States. The patent application in question is only eligible for the PPH program if no substantive examination has occurred in the United States. No additional US Patent Office fees are associated with the PPH program. It is a bilateral world, so getting your patent(s) to issue in close proximity might be in your interest as you work to establish your global brand.

6.5 Petitions to make special (SP)

A petition to make special can take the application out of turn. This can be done if (1) at least one of the inventors is older than age sixty-five, (2) a request is made by the head of a government agency, (3) the patent relates to the environment, (4) the patent relates to the development of energy, or (5) the patent relates to counterterrorism. Each of these cases is related to your existent circumstances.

7. Fundamentals of changing the prosecution conversation

7.1 Prosecution basics and what to expect

This section includes the nuances of prosecution. You may be told that with all of the funky reasoning behind patent claims and (weaselly) known "counterarguments" to objections you will no doubt get rejected on the first office action. When traversing such a rejection, you will be told that if you are allowed into the "argument room" with a resistant examiner, it's a recipe for disaster. You should let patent counsel lead, iteratively traverse the examiner to wear him down, and if an interview is decided on, handle it without you. Assuredly, this is when the prosecution costs will double or triple the drafting and filing costs. As a point of guidance, it is the Schwartz Method's constructive advice that the lead inventor be the critical resource in first understanding any rejection before substantive work on the traversal is done by patent counsel. There is every reason to enable the inventor to be in the fray as it can be postured in a way that inspires the cohort team as well as supports a traversal response that is direct and sensible, and that the cohort team can positively argue in an interview. If push comes to shove, it still may be practical to file a petition to traverse a final rejection by the examiner with the examiner's supervisor or with a PTO board of petition assessors.

7.2 When patent counsel asks you if you even want to proceed

When the going gets tough here, you may even hear from patent counsel, something along the lines of: Do you really need this claim or this part of the patent? Do you even need the patent at all? If you must have it, let us get it for you, despite the resistance from the examiner. We will make sure to get you some of your rights, so stand by. At the end of the day, even if counsel is triumphant under circumstances like this, you will end up with either a mess of a file wrapper, showing all of the flaws in your patent, or with amended claims that water down your monopoly scope and undermine your business model.

7.3 When the innovator takes the lead in the prosecution gambit

It is the right and an opportunity for the invention team to draw the line in the sand and make the arguments for the traversal. The only reason you will be able to change this part of the prosecution conversation is if you drafted DIAAY with the economical and proven Schwartz Method (or some other equivalent methodology of which I am not aware). If you did, you are best prepared to know what you can hope to achieve during early prosecution and you can control the process, making an assessment of any rejections before futile work is allowed to proceed and be paid for. The reality is that if you had a viable invention and you used the Schwartz Method, then you de-risked for fatals before filing and any rejections will be technically amendable without adding new matter. When you can do this, you will preserve your filing date.

7.4 How it works from the inside-out

The key in any response is to stick with a positive and inspiring answer, allowing the examiner to finally understand the invention and the claim. The key is to get the examiner to support the allowance and make a favorable report, along with issuing a notice of allowable matter. That is a rewarding triumph that unifies the cohort team and is worth its weight in gold. Not only do the applicants get what they believe they deserve, they understand the published claims' scope and can assist with infringers downstream, again taking the hard first look at any situation before substantive work is done that ups the patent spend.

I liken the prosecution phase to the "Rube Goldberg" shambles, when one action leads to the next undesirable and irreversible reaction, ultimately ending in a laughable calamity. Here, if the applicant and their cohort team let this chain reaction play out, it's going to be an expensive walk of shame and there will be blame in the game. The slippery slope here is the aspect where patent counsel did the critical claim language defining the broadest scope, using a detailed description that ambiguously supports the claims, then gets into a lengthy prosecution defending their arguments, only to suffer the consequences of overreaching. The patent spending is made on both ends of that candle, leaving nothing to hold when the wicks burn to their ends.

The way to handle prosecution at the lowest cost is to do it almost all yourself, which means that the cohort team documents and archives the prior art found along the way, with clear arguments as to why the new invention patents over it, then forms the draft of the IDS prior to submitting it to patent counsel, let alone to the patent examiner. If you always file an IDS with every application, you will be giving the examiner a pitch on your case for patentability. Even though you are not required to search, and the IDS is not required at the filing date, not preparing, and submitting one is ill advised. If you hear that you can file without search and without an IDS in a "rush your patent application to the altar", rest assured your utility patenting workflow is broken.

All in all, there will be a point in your process when you incrementally assess prior art, and it can, must, and should be early in your consideration to proceed with any formal UCD. Do this before approving any outside patent spending you will eventually have to make on the pathway. I covered some of these considerations in the section on drafting, when the TSM iterative sequence of steps is used to perfect the P-E. The more you iterate on the P-E during drafting, the less you will iterate with the examiner during prosecution, saving up to 70 percent of your overall patent spend. If you are burdened by a flawed utility patent workflow that relies too early and in excess on outside resources to do your representing and defense during the early and critical steps after filing, you will overpay for your largest.

7.5 Be responsive and be positive

Typically, any office action will stipulate the response interval, typically one to three months, unless you used one of the other filing options. If you made a clerical error, you will typically get thirty days to correct technicalities. Substantive rejections will be permitted a three-month period to respond. It is possible to get an extension by the timely payment of a fee, but only do this if it's a situation that is unintentional and unavoidable, like a death in the family of the lead inventor who is a key player in making the traversal. If you want the examiner to remain engaged in a constructive way, do what the examiner asks and respond on time. When you do, you will win in the long run. Remember that the examiner is rated and paid on his through-put. If you protract your prosecution for any reason, there could be an unexpected consequence to this assuredly you will not like. You could risk radicalizing the examiner into a hard, intransigent, fatal rejection. Examiners are human, and they have motivations that are potentially at odds with your goals. It's not complicated—do what you're asked to do and do it on time.

Contrary to what you may hear, it's not complicated or difficult to prepare a response. It's actually a sobering experience. The traversing arguments can be accompanied by any amendments to the claims, if that is what you decide you have to do.

If you must amend the specification to fix something, be very careful. A word in a glossary for an element of your P-E might have been used differently in two places in a specification (specifications have lots of words), and a reference to that key word, spelled incorrectly in a claim, can cause a rejection on rule 112, antecedent reference. That's fixable without adding new matter—it's a correction. On the other hand, if you left out a reference to an element in the context of your identification of the nonobviousness (inventive step), and the reference, even if inserted in an amendment, doesn't do what you define as your unexpected behavior, because you got the P-E wrong, and you're trying to shoehorn in either the specification, or worse the figures, to meet the claimed language. You are not going to come out the other side in good health.

You can, but should not at all cost, amend the detailed description or figures with new matter. If you do (as in the negative example I just gave), you will be cited for adding new matter. If this is done in order to secure a stronger claim or to improve the scope of the claim, that's a no-no. If you do, you may need to refile. Under some circumstance, if the changes (amendments) are allowed, it's possible to file a continuation in part including the new matter (see the patent tactics section), but you will be assigned a new filing date (priority date), and you may risk your priority filing on whatever claim is ultimately allowed.

If there is a competitor in this race, their priority date could unexpectedly precede yours if they filed right the first time, even if they technically filed after you. I cover how to avoid this risk in the drafting and patent tactics sections.

The iteration of new rejections and/or acceptances ultimately results in a progression, and an outcome of either a nonfinal office action (for which you will be given an opportunity to reply/traverse) or a final office action. Final rejections occur in a sequence of unacceptable traversals and the final rejection. Final rejections can be appealed. This entire process has the real potential for coloring your file wrapper sad.

The holy grail is the issuance of a notice of allowance, if and when the patent examiner understands and accepts your traversals, placing your application "in condition for allowance."

7.6 Summary conversation change pointers

In summary, each time the examiner issues an office action, the responsibility to reply returns to the applicant. Here is the rub—you run the risk of deep frustration with this virtual iteration in which you are blocked at the pass. If you are relying solely on paid-for patent services to engage in this often times gruesome exchange, it will get very expensive. If the process lasts three years including up to three replies (note that for your filing fee you are allowed just so many bites at the apple—that is, examiner efforts in actions to assess your merits), that can quickly multiply to $15,000 or more if you're not careful. If you have to file for an extension of prosecution, and the game goes into extra innings, you are going to have to dig even deeper to secure your golden crown.

You may hear, "Do you really want to persist in this? If you must, we can probably get something." That is a real dilemma if you let things get to that place, because that is an ugly reality you never want to experience. That's the bad dream that wakes you up at three in the morning when you realize you added one too many elements to your invention blowing up your novelty, or that your enablement doesn't work when you restructure its description with different elements.

You may be told that in budgeting for prosecution, expect the cost to be one, two, or three times the cost of preparation and filing, and that it's good news if you choose to abandon because you can stop the bleeding. In reality, this situation is fraught with a fundamental conflict of interest if you did not control the drafting and prosecution. Why? Simple: if your patent resource did a poor job on the preparation (for which you may have paid dearly without full appreciation of the flaws), then gainfully but unsuccessfully argues the traversals (with unpredictable money spent), they will be paid on both ends of that candle as it burns, leaving you nothing to hold. Don't let this happen to you.

In the end, you may be told this story up front, along with the explanation that the traversal responses will be a complex mixture of legal and technology arguments, positioning, and amendments that can only be prepared by a utility patenting expert. If you take my advice here and use the Schwartz Method to de-risk your patent application, you will be able not only to self-manage the final approval of the draft patent application and its claim scope but also to administer to the substantive work in developing any arguments to reverse rejections. This is the key to saving big money, and also the key to achieving real patent quality with SCA.

When it comes to the legal construct of estopple for your application, it applies to any of the arguments, actions, and positions you took during prosecution, all of which became part of your file wrapper. The provision limits downstream interpretation of that file wrapper's contents for a granted patent. What does this mean? The most important guidance I can provide is to make sure you never say anything negative about your patent application that could be interpreted to restrict the scope of well-supported claims (don't undersell your innovation). If what you said or did results in what might be interpreted as a restriction on the scope of a claim to be issued later, it might allow someone else to practice the claim with their product, invite an infringement challenge, and then prevail over you in any related action. This will add to your expenses with what I call downstream risk dollars, since litigation of any form will nearly always require patent counsel that practices in the state where proceedings are held, and in front of the court where the litigation will be aired.

Even though any effort to limit the scope of the claim after allowance is prevented by estoppel (stopping the debate), it is permissible to reinterpret the file wrapper, arguing for the restriction and avoidance of infringement. You may be told this is why you should not attempt to handle patent prosecution yourself; however, I would advise the exact opposite. If the applicant is IP savvy (reference the learning and application of IP-BC's the Schwartz Method/BBT), then the kind of response will be exactly the one that supports the most suitable interpretation of the claim scope. When the dust settles, and the only thing to consider in establishing the monopoly rights is the file wrapper and the issued claims. You'll see that it's not really as complicated as it sounds. If you do all the hard work before filing, you will reap the benefits of a clean file wrapper during prosecution and a strongly supported claim that defies reinterpretation.

8.0 Fundamentals of changing the conversation about after allowance considerations

8.1 Patentability vs. patent infringement

We covered how patentability was comprised of two dimensions during examination: (1) patent eligibility and (2) innovation novelty and nonobviousness. During examination, novelty and nonobviousness depend on the claims and how they relate to the prior art cited (either in your IDS or in independent findings of the examiner during his/her mythical person search to debunk your invention).

Patent infringement opinions are different. Here, claims have the personality of a different beast. This is not double talk. Patent infringement is a post-issuance consideration—someone has a published patent, and someone else is practicing what looks like the invention, as patented by another (i.e., you). Understanding when that claim analysis is done for each of these two considerations makes double the sense. Yet even when you get it, there are still fuzzy dimensions to the use of claims when determining patentability in comparison to infringement.

Fuzziness can turn on something as challenging as how well you searched in the first place. How complete were you in identifying prior art and claiming over it in the first place. Fuzziness can depend on your ability to establish all of the elements in an alleged infringing object and how you compare those elements to at least one claim that reads on the minimum set of elements in that object.

Here's another way to reason through this. If we leave the basic factors considered for patentability of an invention behind us for a moment and use the critical juncture of issuance to explain the difference between patentability and patent infringement, it can help sort this out. Again, at first glance, patentability and patent infringement appear to have similarities, but in actuality they have very different meanings, and it is important to identify and be clear about those differences. In the section on patentability, we were faced with passing-through rules 101 (eligibility), 102 (novelty), and 103 (nonobviousness). There, any reference with any description that manifests your invention could be used to reject your claimed invention.

8.2 What it means to infringe

With infringement, the criteria turn on the claims in a different way. For a product that is found to infringe the claim in an issued patent, that product, process, method, transformation, etc., must contain all of the elements of at least one claim of the granted patent. This is true even if in the detailed description of your patent you discuss the possibility of a variety of other embodiments of which this identified infringing one matches. If the claims at the end of your patent specify a limitation—that is, in your requirement for the thing to work, it comprises specifically named elements, and the alleged infringing item doesn't include that element, even if it solves the same problem, then there is no patent infringement. In other words, if theirs is simpler and basically still gets the job done, there is no infringement. In this case, the scope of the claim will come into play. This is where you will hear how critical it is to have your claim drafted by a patent professional, and to a degree that is true, but if you know the English language, understand the principle of scope, and are willing to discover some of the special words always used in legalese claims, then that professional can be you (DIAAY). For example, one of those special words is *at least*. You wouldn't think there's anything special about *at least*. However, if the wording uses, for example, "at least glotch" in the claim being used to try the infringement opinion, it would mean that an object with your glotch would likely infringe that claim.

It can get a little more complicated when you think about whether the product you found, and that you believe infringes your patent, also has a patent on it. You can see how that might work. When you have an issued patent with your claims, your right is to stop someone else. Your patent doesn't actually guarantee you the right to get out of jail free with a freedom to operate card. Your issued patent claims do not automatically guarantee that a product you make that embodies your invention doesn't infringe the patent of another, in particular if their patent has a filing date for a supported claim that precedes yours.

8.3 If and when it happens – how to think about it and what to do

Developing a sixth sense for how to interpret these situations in real time can be enhanced by understanding how the old rules worked in the pre-AIA days. As with any complex domain, looking at the rules and then understanding how they are used or changed to improve them will always shed new insight. In the old days of first to invent, if each of you and your competitors' patent applications were routed through the same (or related) art group, at the same time, but with different examiners, the examiners would conduct an internal due diligence audit/search and if they found two patent applications with substantially similar inventions, they would conduct what was called an interference. This would all be done inside the patent office before issuance (or litigation), and a determination would be made as to who invented first. If, as in the case I presented earlier, both products did have patents applied for, and they both issued without being handled in an interference proceeding internally at the patent office during examination, then if there was infringement after issuance, ostensibly the infringer would be the one with the later filing date. There are nuances to this situation when it comes to freedom to operate if you do infringe but were first to invent. The issue is in regard to evading the payment of royalties to the other party. If and only if you can legally prove that you invented first, you would be allowed to practice (freedom to operate) without paying royalties, but the other party would keep its monopoly rights with any others.

This entire subject and the act of considering infringement is a legal pothole everyone hopes to avoid. At the same time, if the situation arises, level heads must prevail, and that means that the lead inventor should participate in the conversation about the alleged infringement and weigh in on the physical comparisons first, before other cohorts run around like chickens with their heads cut off. Take a deep breath and use your smartest internal resources to make a first assessment. At the point legal counsel needs to get involved, it should be critically clear that there even is an infringement at all.

8.4 Infringement can be even more complex

In point of summary, now that you understand what it means to have been granted a patent (meaning a patent application was filed, it was examined by a patent office, the examiner deemed the invention patentable, claims in that patent were granted, and the patent published), it's important to restate that you do not instantly get an affirmative right to use or practice the invention. What you really have is kind of an inverted right. Stated using the legal meaning of a patent grant, you as the patent owner, have the right to exclude others from making, using, selling, or importing any product or service that embodies your claimed invention. To keep your patent valid, you must assert your rights against any alleged offender, or you will lose your right to stop them or anyone else.

A case might arise where another was granted a patent that covers some portion of your product or service with an earlier filing date than you, which would prevent you from having the freedom to operate with that piece of the jigsaw puzzle. If to make, use, and sell your product, you need to make, use, and sell a component someone else owns, then you can't proceed in the market unless you establish bilateral rights through a legal instrument. Often, the tactic turns into a strategy insofar as negotiating a license to make, use, or sell their component (the one you are infringing) means getting into a business relationship with them. This could be contentious, or it could be collaborative. The key in sharing this perspective on this part of the conversation is to enable you to control your conversation about the future. If this turns on your business strategy, then that's your right and obligation to get fixed, not your patent counsel's. The situations I have seen where two competing attorneys take the issue to the mats usually end poorly. If a situation arises, finding a mutual business goal first as part of the owner's process will usually result in a less acrimonious legal wrangle.

The ugly fight will occur if they have a valid claim and won't license you but instead decide to try and stop you with an injunction designed to prevent you from proceeding with your commercial objectives. Here, typically as a maneuver to get around either a threatened (cease and desist letter) or a granted injunction (one put in place in a court of law in the state in which the suit was filed), the offending player will try to invalidate the patent claim and/or the patent that is being asserted for the cease and desist or injunction.

This is where the use of the Schwartz Method to read their patent, interpret their file wrapper (you have to get it by requesting it from the patent office), analyze it, and debunk it can come into play. The Schwartz Method can be used to reverse engineer the scope of the claims in a competing application by applying the Schwartz Method UPL rules and GP to that patent. It turns out that being able to read a competing patent is as important a skill as being able to use the Schwartz Method to draft an airtight patent application. IP-BC ADVANCED shares a good example of how this can be done with a robotics invention from a prominent robotics company. In that example, the patent and claim is very strong, and the use case shows how the Schwartz Method uncovers that in the "reverse reading process."

8.5 Summary conversation change points

Each situation bears a very close look by the owners first. There are as many variations on how to use a patent offensively or defensively as there are stars in the sky, so knowing the inside-out rubric can help deconstruct any situation before it gets ugly. The conversation-changing message here is to do careful analysis up front, including the business trade-offs for the parties, to establish alternatives and identify the least costly pathway to avoid or minimize conflict. Business executives can usually do this by identifying and considering the truth versus the fake news about what is really afoot. Once there is mistrust in this part of the patent journey, it's going to get expensive. I've heard at least one patent counsel brag to an audience that when there is litigation, it's their specialty, and they run upstairs every morning to defend their clients. I don't doubt that for a minute, and I'm also sure that it's a belief held by others and, further, that they are really good at litigation. No one likes a lawyer until they need one. The point here is not to run amok and try to do this all on your own, but rather to sort it out well before you need to ask for substantive legal tasking to fight it out. When the call for legal help is made, and you are defining the engagement agreement with counsel, proceeding with all the known facts on the table first will change this conversation. Knowing what and how to ferret out the facts is the game changer. In a case like this, having an experienced patent counsel may become a critical component of DIAAY.

In summary, the lesson learned here is to keep in mind how the two considerations work in real time by looking at them in the sequence in which they occur. During examination, finding on an invention as patentable over relevant prior art (alone or in combination) requires looking at everything the prior art teaches. The examiner is allowed to consider and use anything in the prior art reference (if a patent, the detailed description, the summary, the figures, etc. even if not the claims) to determine whether it renders your invention obvious—that is, whether it teaches your invention. In other words, what is used when considering patentability during examination is information described anywhere in the art reference, whether or not it was part of a reviewed and allowed patent claim. In contrast, the patent infringement analysis looks only at the "Claims" section of a granted patent. To infringe a patent, a product or service must contain all of the elements of at least one claim of the granted patent. This is why you need to do the hard work and understand all the variations of your invention when developing the P-E. Those alternatives will be documented in your IDPAW as part of the Schwartz Method and they will come into play here, rather than taking you by surprise, or relying on another expensive post-issuance process to unravel what is going on. When you work on your layman's claims during the second and third cycles in the Schwartz Method (refer to the IP-BC/ADVANCED PRACTITIONER thirty-day do-it-yourself challenge), you will draft claim sets that have protective scope to capture other variations of your invention that could hurt you in the market if they were allowed to be made, used, and sold by another. Change this conversation by making sure patent counsel doesn't sell you on their ability to make sure you have the broadest scope, because if the scope is off the edge, you will have hell to pay as others enter the market and you have to stop them all. The trick is to make sure that when your layman's claim is converted to legalese during final preparation and before filing, that you patent over the prior art you or the examiner may uncover and use against you during patent prosecution and that you select the scope you need for your business model in relationship to your known competitors.

That's really all you can do—the rest will be determined by time and the mythical person, deep-grind searches that will follow your market success. Here again, experience will show that the claim scope sought is intertwined with your business objectives. Why? If your business objective is licensing, and you want to license everyone (nonexclusively), then if you can, you may decide to seek a supported claim with the broadest scope so everyone will infringe and have to come to you for a license. If your objective is to make, use, and sell it, and you know exactly what the better mousetrap is, then getting a narrower claim with the scope that ensures your freedom to operate, but also doesn't require you to stop the other lesser than equals could be the way to go.

When considering claim scope, it is a slippery slope. If during prosecution, the examiner finds that the claims are too broad (showing art he refused to ignore, which he or she applies to your claim and issues rejections on rule 102 [nonobviousness]), then an interview between the applicant and the examiner may be warranted. Depending on who prevails, your scope may be adjusted. One possible way to get an indication of merit and a claim that's good enough is if you can both agree on the addition of a limitation to your claims that narrows its scope, so that the examiner no longer holds the prior art against you in order to distinguish your claimed invention from the cited prior art (for either rule 101 [novelty] or, more challenging, rule 102 [nonobviousness]). Enough on this as I suspect you do get it and, further, that my message about your role in preparing and then changing the conversation is clear. Do the hard work beforehand, and you will minimize your downstream risk.

Lots of things can happen during this stage. To reiterate, if you are accused of patent infringement, make the preliminary analysis yourself. If you find it hard to make the case that your product doesn't infringe the claims of the plaintiffs' patent, then your next step may need to find a way to invalidate their patent. This is when you will need to search again with a vengeance and review your findings along with deconstructing their file wrapper. If you were doing your own slow-grind search the whole while as part of your improved IP workflow, then you may be on the edge of your seat, ready to pounce. Using artificial intelligence at this point is cost-effective and well advised, since you know exactly what they are asserting. Finding art that dispenses with the claims they are asserting on you as well as tearing into their file wrapper will help you prevail if it's meant to be. It's worth looking at everything at this point, even technicalities. It's doubtful that they don't have patent-eligible subject matter, but it is likely that they did some stupid things like not providing a sufficient written description (ambiguous), not referencing the terms consistently (antecedent reference), or not showing a best mode with technical enablement that teaches how it works.

On your pathway to patentship, if the names of critical elements in your claims can be sustained in the face of these forces seeking to unhook you, then you will get acclaim on the walk of fame instead of having to face the walk of shame (abandonment).

9.0 Now for more angles on patent tactics and strategies

9.1 Understand what the lawyers are saying – then change the conversation

First, always be thinking about the type of patent application you will be seeking as you prepare your IDPAW entries. This will help you simplify the first step in your process and avoid being asked to supply an invention disclosure to counsel too soon. If you are asked for an invention disclosure document as part of the engagement of a patent professional, you will want to turn the tasking inside out and tie down the work product with a UCD. It will help to use this Part-2 in combination with (at least) IP-BC/ADVANCED. If you follow the Schwartz Method and the BBT I teach, then you will have a non-provisional UCD that you or your patent counsel can automatically translate into a UCPA at the end of INTERVAL 4 of the Schwartz Method.

9.2 To be or not to be? Pursue a patent at all?

Let's keep talking about patents by looking at critical tactic and strategy considerations as a way to shed even more light on this complex domain. Now that you can see how the patenting gambit works, the question of whether you should patent at all can be revisited with the goal of sharing additional insight. It's a question that I implicitly ask you to answer with each step of the iterative IDPAW formation sequence in the Schwartz Method. If you honestly ask this question over and over during the pre-drafting process in your effort to compose a viable UCD, you will be in a very good position to know the answer in time. I call this 20-20 hindsight. Your hard work will in fact help you increase the probability that you will fulfill your vision by your ability to see the future. If you get a sick feeling in your stomach about the answer to this question, that may prove just as valuable. When you make the assessment, you will see ways to incrementally change the direction of your innovation, completely change your innovation, or adjust your business model. This could result in helping you partner with another based on your strengths and capabilities. You will always be evaluating your business plan and whether your claimed innovation will be the quintessential enabler. This will open new doors and close others.

9.3 Other things you may be told and how to respond

You may be told that the patenting process is long, complicated, and expensive and this should give you pause. In point of fact with the Schwartz Method, as you move through your product development cycle with the BBT set of guiding principles, you are always pre-drafting. With my approach, the process of preparing and filing a patent application is a translation step, so it's actually not complicated, not long, and not expensive. Yes, the prosecution may take time, but here again, if you used the Schwartz Method, you won't get caught in the wringer of a protracted series of compromising office action rejections. When push comes to shove, if you believe you need to create a barrier to entry as part of your business development game plan, then putting a patent application on file (with a great claim) will give you one simple offensive weapon for a reasonable price—by putting "patent pending" on your product or service, you will warn others to stay clear. This window may be short or long depending on many factors.

9.4 One-year rule considerations

I mentioned the one-year rule—no one will see your stuff for a year if you keep the claims in your provisional application confidential. You can extend this interval if you decide not to file internationally, stipulate this at the time of filing your non-provisional application, and keep the claims confidential. At the end of the day, anyone either licensing or competing with you will only care about your claims. If you don't stipulate you are not filing internationally, your patent application will be published as is with its claims for all to see. No matter, if you did the hard work and have a great patent on file, then the benefit in placing "patent pending" on your go-to products will give you an early opportunity to boost cash flow from licensing royalties or product sales revenue. The warning sign to potential competitors cannot and should not be underrated. At the end of the day, based on granted claims, you can and must enforce your rights by noticing them and then suing any actual infringer for patent infringement (doing your own assessment first) in federal court. This is the only way to get an injunction against them to prevent them from making, using, selling, or importing the infringing products. Patents are the preferred way to protect product revenues and to educate your product marketing department and your customers about your value proposition.

9.5 Using provisional applications vs. non-provisional applications

You can change the conversation simply knowing that with your first patent filing for your invention using a provisional patent application, that you can put "patent pending" on your product. At the same time, I make a cautionary note here. Follow the Schwartz Method GP rule and include at least one claim in it, covering your invention, and you'll be in a stronger position. The provisional application is only a placeholder for your filing date. If your specification doesn't support a properly scoped claim when you flip it to a non-provisional application, you are sure to risk losing your provisional filing date. This would happen if at the end of one year, when you went to flip it to a non-provisional application, you discovered that the claim you now want or have to have is not supported by the specification you filed in the provisional application. If you have to amend the provisional application on filing, the date for that claim will get the new filing date (rules 111, 112, 113). Examination will then proceed on that application. A provisional application offers an offensive posture during the product development life cycle, but it's much more of a weapon if you used the Schwartz Method to draft it, especially if you are trying to raise go-to-market money. You may be told that if you gave a solid invention disclosure to a competent patent counsel in an effort to convince your investors that you have gotten patent protection, you may be in for a rude awakening. In reality, if your goal is to proceed with a non-provisional application, you will have to flip whatever you filed in the provisional application filed within one year, or that filing will automatically go abandoned. So, in order to claim priority from the filing date of your provisional patent application, it better be right the first time.

In summary, you can only really flip it if you had the right claim and you have not added any new matter. The tactic of going to market with the provisional application pending can be praised as a way to be an early mover, but just know that the others will instantly be alerted to your efforts, and the race to patent will heat up. The real competitors will be motivated to accelerate their patent filings if they haven't filed already. This is why with IP SAVVYS, I continue to repeat the need to get the filing you seek to file first right the first time.

Remember, the provisional application only establishes a filing priority date for your attempt at being the first-to-file. It is not examined, and it will be automatically abandoned after one year if you don't flip it. With a Schwartz Method, drafted provisional application, you could pay the additional fee as a non-provisional application and file that way on day one. Some patent counsel will suggest that you should always start with the provisional application. Sometimes however, this is akin to kicking the can down the road. If you file with a non-provisional patent application first, then you will be off to the examination races from the starting gun. You won't be taking a test lap around the track. It is still okay to use the provisional application with a properly scoped claim; then, when you flip it, if you are filing globally, you can file your PCT application at that time and claim the priority date of that original provisional application, as long as you haven't added new matter.

9.6 Non-provisional applications and foreign filing

The non-provisional application is required for foreign filing. You can always file your non-provisional application in a PCT application as your first application if you don't use the one-year rule to flip the US filing and file conterminously with the PCT. Whichever office you filed your non-provisional application in first will likely be the first to examine it. Also, since there is deferred filing for non-provisional applications at the country stage for each country you selected, you might be able to use this time to form license arrangements or partnerships in those countries in order to balance off the translation expenses and other patent office fees required to get the patents validated in those countries.

9.7 Patent value

Patents can provide value in a number of different ways. It may not be possible to contemplate the true value of your asset during patent drafting because you won't know your full exclusion rights. Your business team will likely be modeling what your market potential is on a spectrum of claim scope, as that will tie directly back into the product line and marketing strategy. When considering the potential value of an issued patent, I insist on using the Schwartz Method to de-risk your application before filing so that when it does issue, you will have a clean file wrapper and a clear claim scope. I call patents that issue this way assets with real SCA. When you get one like that, the patent's worth can be evaluated and/or wielded in a number of ways.

Be seen as an innovator. When you differentiate, you can conquer markets if you have identified an economical must-have way to solve a pervasive and recognized problem. Product marketing will also benefit from IP-BC and the Schwartz Method. They can all take the INTERMEDIATE LEVEL so that they understand what has been accomplished with the patent and how to read it. Yes, having an IP savvy marketing department is part of the game plan when using the Schwartz Method. With a properly crafted marketing message centered around the egregious limitations of the competition, new streams of revenue from product sales will substantiate the patent value.

Partnering and licensing: If your goal is solely to license, and you will not be making, using, and selling, then crisply scoped claims will show you the white space you fit into your target market(s), as well as the companies to seek out as prospects to take a license for your patent, in return for a royalty. Patents with strong dependent claims will garner more royalties, as they will cover variations of the embodiments made, used, and sold by your licensees—the basis on which the royalties are calculated. You may be picking partners to complete the solution, by identifying compatible licensees. It may make sense to offer an exclusive license, but the terms in contracts for these usually require you to indemnify your licensee against the risk of infringement and other downstream business challenges. Often your licensing prospects will not sign confidentiality agreements. Why? They will not want to compromise their own internal efforts to patent so as not to have to license and pay royalties. This is not an easy street. In fact, it's a very challenging street if you seek to license nonexclusively, since your licensees become competitors of each other. In other cases, your clients will license in order to get the drop on you, in turn filing their own patent on their own non-infringing product and becoming your competitor. They may even be the ones that seek an *ex parte* petition to invalidate your patent and make the exact product you licensed them. Fun and games? Not really. With my company, I did license nonexclusively and walked this talk. This is one of the reasons I hope the sage advice offered in this book will help you avoid some of the potholes I had to navigate around. Writing a nonexclusive license hinges on ensuring your licensee that you will not prevent them from owning and controlling claims in the domain you are in that you don't otherwise own now (i.e., at the time the license is taken) or at any time in the future. A good licensing counsel will take the Schwartz Method, read, and understand your patent, and know how many teeth to put into the contracts.

9.8 More considerations – stopping others, protecting freedom to operate

Stopping others from making if you are making and selling yourself: If you intend to use your patent(s) offensively, then you will be sending out a lot of cease and desist letters, engaging on the infringement opinion conversation, and potentially flipping an adversary into a licensee, especially if you can establish repurposed niches where you will not be directly competing. Sometimes, the more the merrier. There is always a larger market when customers have a reasonable number of alternatives, if the choices offer slightly different value.

Protecting your freedom to operate: Your patent claim(s) can protect you from others alleging that you infringed their patent. Here, a mindful assessment of who did it first and who owns what might be helpful (see the video vignette "Abbot and Costello: Who's On First" in IP-BC Entry to get a humorous view of how complicated infringement issues could be, if you're all not seeking one unequivocable truth using the same language). The Schwartz Method teaches UPL, so that you can read anyone else's patent without having to have an attorney do that first. You do it first, then have that conversation after your own assessment.

Seven hundred-pound gorilla: If you truly identified a discontinuity in the market, and the scope of your initial claims gets you the market share to fuel your gambit, you will have the advantage as you will see other aspects of the niche you can develop with complementary and protectable innovations. In this way you can build a patent portfolio that can expand your economic clout in the white space you've chosen. This is also called a Blue Ocean, as you define your territorial rights in an expansive manner. When I first patented what I referred to as the "surface" computer in my first claim in my 1989 patent, I realized that the innovation I discovered was not only a packaging concept but also a new form of mechanical book that could get children more organized in the old analog sense. I was very early with my vision for surface computers (it would take nearly twenty more years for the technology I envisioned would become feasible). However, in my mechanical bookbinding space, I was not only able to get seven more patents on my surface, but I also identified additional innovations that allowed me to get twenty-seven more patents on at least five complementary products. I licensed all of them globally and at the peak of my business efforts, I had more than one thousand people at five licensees making, using, and selling my products across big-box stores in North America. Our licensees, if put in one room and weighed, would qualify as the seven hundred-pound gorilla. I was a gorilla maker.

9.9 Patent tactics: The filing document packet (DOC PAK)

Filing: You are examined on merits after you file. You may be told that since the filing packet requires specific and complicated forms that must be completed in nuanced ways, including forming the package and using the most currently published fees, that this step is also the province of patent counsel. I have a section on filing in IP-BC that covers the procedural steps in an effort to inform you about the minimal things needed and what someone must do—tedious as it might be—to get the package completed and ready for your application to be put on file. There's a good checklist for this part of the process. I share a sample set of proper forms for a provisional application and show you how to complete them correctly as the last step before the prosecution phase on your pathway to patentship. Following my guiding principles, you are actually prepared with everything you need as you develop your IDPAW, so that at the time your claims are perfected and you're ready to file, you have all the information to submit, all at the lowest stress levels. This part of the utility patenting effort is not rocket science, and you can do it yourself if you follow the checklist in the course (another part of the guiding principles). As it turns out, it's a lot less complicated than filing a tax return because all you have to do is fill in the blanks and not lie. There's no strategy on how to prepare the filing packet—it's cut and dried.

9.10 The one-year rule revisited one more time

The one-year rule offers an opportunity to protect your invention with a non-provisional patent in the United States after its first public disclosure. You have one year to file your non-provisional patent application on it. Remember that if you use a provisional application as a placeholder to say, "patent pending," you still have to file the non-provisional application within one year after making the innovation public. Also remember that the opportunity to protect that same invention in certain countries—in particular China—is immediately lost upon any public disclosure or public sale before filing in that country. If you are going global, then you must stipulate that at the time of filing, and you must file before any such public disclosure (e.g., non-confidential investor pitches, publication on the Web using crowdfunding, innovation monetary reward competitions, pre-announcing to your customers with sales and marketing literature, publication of white papers). Other countries may have some form of grace period as well, as with the PCT countries. Another overriding consideration, intertwined with any of the public disclosure, is becoming your own prior art and losing your right to file in certain foreign countries. Additionally, you will need to have an efficient, flawless process if you want to be first-to-file.

9.11 More on AIA, first to file, and alternative game plans

As I explained earlier, the United States used to have a first-to-invent system, but on March 16, 2013, the United States harmonized its patent laws with international conventions and adopted the first-to-file system.

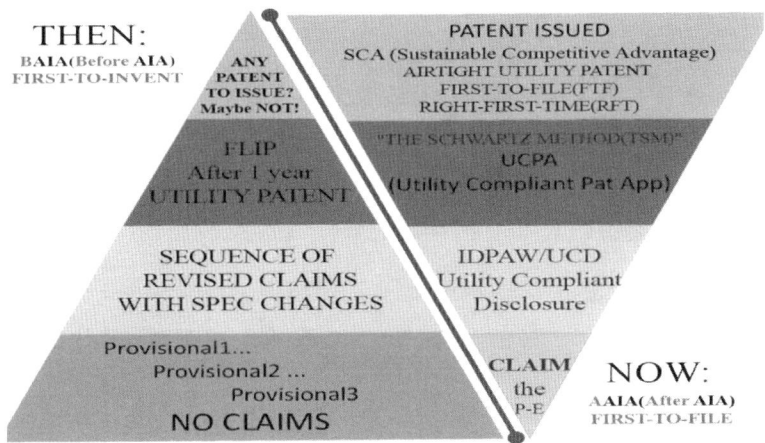

Fig13. Before AIA and after AIA – the pyramid is upside down

In the days before AIA, an inventor could use any form of documentation, typically a witnessed and signed page in a lab or inventor notebook, and if needed (due to an interference proceeding, or in a downstream lawsuit), submit bona fide documentation on a date of conception (to whoever was in the loop—that is, the patent office or a federal district court), in an effort to establish priority and secure monopoly rights. The examiner or judge on the case would take this evidence and use it to determine who was the first to invent. Today, the filing you secure with either your provisional or non-provisional application, so long as it has a supported claim in the detailed description and conforms to the MPEP rules for the patent format, will determine the monopoly holder for that claimed P-E. So, with the first-to-file system, you may be given false confidence by being told you can put the label "patent pending" on your product with any form of patent application, provisional or non-provisional, for the entire time it is pending. I admonish that it is ill advised to file a bible provisional without a claim as the basis for putting "patent pending" on your product, even though you legally can. I have covered this from a number of angles, and I'm restating it here as part of how you should choose to change the conversation.

On filing your non-provisional application in the United States, if you do use a PCT application, it will serve as your international placeholder allowing you to delay filing in any participating foreign country where you seek patent protection. You will have a total of thirty months from your earliest priority date (which may be your US provisional application) to seek publication. At each point in the foreign application process, you will use a foreign agent to handle the paperwork, and this will run into real money, up to $10,000 per country, including translation costs when required. You will get an international examiner who does an independent patentability search and separately reports the results to the applicant. The EPO will report to you, as will each country through their liaison. Typically, an inventor who has an international business opportunity will file a provisional application at the US Patent Office first, in what I call a UCPA. Anyone being told it's okay to use a concept provisional application (what I call the back-of-the-napkin provisional application) should not try to use it to establish an international priority date—period. Don't be lured into the first-to-file argument that it's okay to file a 75 percent complete draft. Why? It's guaranteed that during the product development steps when working on the completion of the product, there will be hard changes that will require different claims and new supporting matter, and this will surely ruin any chance that the priority date of what you thought was your inventive concept will benefit from your earlier filing date. When your non-provisional application is filed, you can't change it during prosecution. If you use the Schwartz Method, you will pursue a patent application on a P-E that is the same as what you claimed one year later. If you don't use the Schwartz Method, then you will need to perfect an alternative method to achieve the same outcome, or you will pay the piper. With all these considerations, if you are going global, the usual tactic is to file a US non-provisional application claiming priority to the provisional application at the one-year mark and not use the delayed window from the PCT to file the international applications at the thirty-month mark. Everything is filed conterminously in order to accelerate prosecution on both fronts. Under this scenario, your US non-provisional application is pending at the same time as the PCT application. Both applications will publish eighteen months from the priority date of the provisional application. With a favorable report from either the US or PCT examination, thirty months from the provisional application priority date you opt in and enter the national/regional phase and each patent agent in each country prepares your country-specific notice of allowance and publication.

9.12 What about trial case law and its impact on your patent claiming

Another tactical issue is the reality that trial cases on issued patents will continue to change what is allowable not only for eligibility but also for novelty and nonobviousness, which will refine the meaning of scope. Enablement considerations also come into play in the case law. My guiding principle in the Schwartz Method is simply this: stay true to your P-E, refine your layman's claim for it, support it with the best mode known to you at the time you file, ensure you completely disclose any critical inventive nature of your enablement that permits the unexpected behavior of your invention, and drive claim scope to a realistic target (for your business model). Do this and you will skirt the squirrely legal traps that create all of the downstream risk. If you are in a nuanced technology classification such as software, there are many well-written assessments of cases such as the "Alice decision" that give further guidance on what is allowable for a computer-based patent application. I cover one aspect of this in IP-BC/ADVANCED with the treatment of the machine or transformation (MOT) test. Here, the idea of tying the software algorithm to a machine and establishing that the process performs a substantive change to the state of the data it is operating on, and does not just perform useless churning, is discussed. I contend that the MOT criteria were part of the fundamental interpretation of MPEP on novelty and the ruling only strengthened the interpretation of novelty and nonobviousness for software. The reason for Alice was the unnatural scope stretch that legal minds put into the claimed software for patents that made them too broad. The nature of this fight emerged in the open-source battles with trolls buying up licensable patents and enforcing them without making anything—just pursuing the collection of royalties. It was and still is a mess and learning about the details is relevant if you are filing software patents. I cover a good bit of this in my blog post on trolls at www.ipboostcamp.com. You may be told that only a patent professional can interpret the different case law rulings, and that knowledge of these interpretations along with others will be the only way to counter and traverse an examiner's rejection, especially for obvious rejections based on prior art. Again, if you stick to your knitting and do the right things in casting your P-E into legal claims supported in the specification of your application, you'll be in a good place when you file. If you have to deal with the nuanced issues during prosecution, the interpretation of the examiner's opinion in the office action will be subject to the same principle I proposed for the infringement allegation. Take a deep breath, read the rejection over and over first, and make sure you understand the examiner's position. He or she may be trying to help you, suggesting what you can do to amend the claim so that it meets the threshold criteria they have been trained to apply. Sure, not all examiners have the same IQ or understand the nuance of law in the same way, but they are your first line of reasoning. So, before you have counsel give you their spin on any such rejection as the basis for taking over the response to office action, potentially deepening the pothole, ask counsel to answer your question about the meaning of the subjective case law being applied and see if what they're telling you makes sense to you. You will typically have three months to respond unless you picked an accelerated pathway. Don't wait until the last minute if you want to handle this situation of rejection and minimize cost and complexity. It is also possible that if you did not use the Schwartz Method, and there is a flaw in the specification that prevents the claimed scope and ultimately is the basis of a final rejection, that it might be the fault of the drafter. In that case, you are paying on both sides of this—not only the cost of the drafting but also the cost of an ill-conceived prosecution that you may well have lost control of. Avoiding FOARS before filing is the guiding principle of IP-BC's Schwartz Method. It's your job to be on top of that concept, and you will prevail even with hotly sought-after technology-based patent applications.

9.13 Patent ownership considerations

Another area for patent tactic considerations is in the area of patent ownership. Often there is more than one inventor, even though there is a lead inventor (the one whose ideation resulted in an actual claim in the patent that is included in the specification as the first claim). When there is more than one inventor, it can get more complicated and legal disputes could arise. Whether it's a sole inventor or many inventors, if they work for the company, my guiding principle is to have them assign all of their rights in the invention to the company for one dollar. I include a section on this in IP-BC when covering the chain of ownership and the title rights in the patent when it's filed. The process of assignment is very straightforward, and the agreement on the nature of ownership is airtight. You will either ask someone to sign one or you will be asked to sign one. Every situation is different, and if the assignment is sought for someone who performed work for hire on the development of the invention, then they should well have been asked to sign such an assignment document before starting work, even if by the laws of your state, their work for hire is de facto owned by the company who contracted them. It is critical to establish clean and unambiguous lines of ownership before filing, and it's part of the patent filing DOC PAK. Lie about this, and you're perpetrating fraud at the patent office—trust me, there will be costly battles to fight, not to mention fines, if you were circumspect about this seemingly obvious consideration. If and when you are doing your IDPAW for the P-E and sharing your invention with a patent professional whom you have selected to finalize your patent application, if they are patent lawyers who have passed the bar and the MPEP test, they are obligated by attorney-client privilege to keep your information a trade secret and they have no ownership rights. If they become co-inventors, this can get a little murky. If that appears to have occurred, whether legally bound or patent agents, I suggest you have them sign your assignment agreement for one dollar anyway, just to be safe. Often counsel will coach the lead inventor to be the sole ideation source. Here again, your discretion will prevail. If you do your own trade secret process and get to the P-E before engaging any outside helpers, you won't have to face this potential conflict of interest.

The whole purpose is to establish a right in ownership for the invention, and when it's a discontinuity maker, it may not involve the improvement of something that existed before. For a nonobvious improvement, you have to see if it's going to be an improvement over something you had before or if it's an improvement over something from another. If it's over your own stuff (i.e., a prior patent you filed, whether pending or issued), your sole objective must be to start the clock over on the patent term; otherwise, you will be "terminally disclaimed"—the duration of your patent will be curtailed by an office action tying your improvement to the original filing date. In any case, with improvements, the chain of title is just as critical, and the claimed improvement must be vetted for the rightful owner.

None of this is really all that complicated. You may be told that patent attorneys, patent agents, or other helpers will use paralegals and other administrative staff members that know how to collect and prepare this type of information. My guiding principle is hand the draft documents to them, filled out first, Then when the filing package is ready, you can audit the papers and make sure that they are right the first time. If you don't, you could get delays in the prosecution because the examiner will not look at your case until it's perfectly compliant with MPEP. MPEP documents tell you exactly what to do, so it's a no-brainer to take this part over in your IP workflow. The Doc Pak filing components will pop out of your process as soon as you've quiesced your first independent claim.

Remember that to DIAAY and to self-manage your IP workflow, if IP counsel says they want an invention disclosure document and gives you a list of wants for the contents, let the alarm bell ring. This can turn into an open door for a sequence of tasks and billing moments that could turn ugly in a heartbeat. You will find that by using the IP-BC UCPA, you can navigate around this pothole. Patent counsel may say they don't understand what an IDPAW, UCD, or UCPA is and that you're not using the same language to communicate, so teach them. In reality, counsel is ultimately doing the exact same thing with the invention disclosure but keeping it to themselves as shamans of the process. When you force the issue and get your helpers speaking as IP SAVVYS, then both client and counsel are on mutual footing and equally organized. I do believe that using my glossary will clear this up and it's an appendix to this book. It's still your responsibility, whether as counsel adopting the Schwartz Method or as a client asking your counsel to use the Schwartz Method, to get everyone on the same page, and this is really the only way to get both the client and the counsel more organized and clearer on who will do what, when, and why.

That's one of the reasons I deliver IP-BC in levels and expose the patent rubric. The course levels are targeted to teach utility patenting based on your IP role, title, and tasking. The trick is not to fall prey to having a ton of heavy MPEP rules, patent counsel admonitions, legal precedents by subject matter area, and explanations that confuse more than they help dumped on you as a fear trigger. Read and reread this book to get your arms around what's about to happen in your mutual team effort to get patents with SCA.

9.14 General guidance pointers

You are going to find a lot of books, guides, and patent office resources about utility patents and their complexity. If you have read and understood *IP Savvy*, then you won't be haloed by the trap where you are shown how you can or will fall into the forbidden zone unless you use patent counsel for the whole process. As you have now discovered, when you apply my innovator perspective on this, the conversation turns on being IP savvy and getting into the IP Zone as a safe place.

In other words, when you hear, see, or read directly or in between the lines "Don't try this at home," I hope you will return to this guide and this course as your antidote to that line of reason. When you hear that you should not bother trying to do it yourself, the end result will be catastrophic, and you should use a good lawyer instead, move ahead with confidence using my DIAAY guidance on the pathway to patentship (sm).

There is always a fine line along the slippery slope that takes you to one side of this argument or the other. Try to use this book as the thin line and the GPS offering you a pathway along your journey down the IP corridor of uncertainty.

As you reread this book and discuss it with your cohorts and patent counsel—that is, for both innovators and patent counsel alike—try to see the other side's point of view, their seemingly conflicting goals, and reset your thinking with each point of information. All parties entering the IP Zone have passionate and willful intentions, skill sets, and gifts with which to achieve their IP goals. This compendium is not a criticism of any one point of view, suggested as being spun from any one of the IP hunters, insomuch as it's a rational attempt to lay them out for dissection, reprocessing, and reformulation. Clever dissection will enable all parties to change their IP conversation so that they can divide the utility patenting tasks and conquer them together. I'm going to follow on here with more of these conversation points and ideas on how to change that aspect of the process.

10. The great debate—summary guidance: He said, she said

10.1 When the games are underway

What you may hear/alternative points of view. I have covered a lot of this with my approach in showing ways to change your utility patenting conversations. Here, I will cover additional angles on conversation changing opportunities along with additional points of consideration. A helpful way will be to break down the intervals of time to before, during and after.

10.2 Before

It's our way or the highway.

You may hear that after you have reviewed the prior art, decided there is something patentable about your invention, and filed an invention disclosure document, you should immediately engage a patent professional to prepare, file, and prosecute your patent application…that it is imperative that you work with a patent professional to do everything. Simply no. If you have read and understood this book and taken IP-BC, you are in control of who to talk to, about what, and when to ask for substantive work to be done.

Intellectual property is abstract.

You may be told that with utility patents, the borders are inherently difficult to identify because the property is described using language and images rather than with physical boundaries. You cannot pick it up and hold it or read a manual describing it.

Yes, the world of utility patenting is complex. At the same time, utility patents are really all about an object of invention, and objects are things with structure and function. In fact, they are very specific representations of what will become familiar as the P-E. To get a patent on an invention that embodies that object, the MPEP requires you to claim and describe a definite representation of that object, in such a manner that it can be made without a lot of experimentation by another—in other words, it is the tip of defining a manual for it. Further, there has been a significant effort to harmonize the global laws in order to clarify what is required in an allowed patent. So, it is not abstract at all, really—patents are a precise, definite, and explicit description of what was an idea as an object of invention. Of course, there are things that can't be patented like abstract ideas not drawn to a machine or thing, or embodiments that can just never work, like perpetual motion machines.

It's going to cost an arm and a leg to get a patent and it will take a long time.

You may be told that it's expensive to draft and even more expensive to prosecute, so you must be sure you know what your business impact will be and how it will justify the dollars you're about to spend. "By the way, we're experts and here's how we get paid. We take a retainer for drafting, our billing rates for senior partners are $$$$ and junior partners $$, so we'll tag-team it to get you the best outcome for your money. Also, you know, we're in business to make a profit, so you will need to understand that. By the way, no matter what the cause of a rejection should there be any (most applications are rejected in the first office action—see the FOARs starter kit), we will be handling all matters of substance at our quoted billing rates (note that prosecution fees can double or triple filing fees)."

When all is said and done, a lot more is usually said than done, and often it is said in vain about the wrong thing and at the wrong time. In other words, no, it doesn't have to be expensive in the sense of worst-case dollar forecasts and expenditures since there is a pathway to gaining a right-first-time utility patent, and the larger part of that can and should be on my DIAAY trajectory that ties the disclosure of an object of invention into the product development life cycle. By keeping it a trade secret, all along, and internally perfecting a UCD, you can proceed quite a ways without one dollar of patent expense. There will be patent expenses, not only internal or outside counsel, but also official patenting fees, but up to the point when, like in a relay race, the baton is passed, during the time you are holding the baton, no legal fees. In this relay race, one aspect that will become evident is that the baton passing can, should, and will be recursive, with the lead runner (in theory and by way of our intention, the innovator who is listed first in the filed patent application) taking the baton over and over again not only through the drafting stage (as you will see the layman construction), but also through the final review before filing, and the first look at office action rejections. How to execute this sequence of events is the core of the IP-BC teachings. The patent professors out there will advocate for their expertise honed over thousands of patents drafted and suggest you turn the project over at the idea stage so that the patent can be drafted and filed before triggering the one-year rule, but if you get the clear picture of how drafting is part of the specification stage in the product development life cycle, then the layman's claim for the P-E will in fact be in hand when the patent drafting is to be done, and that could truly be more like a language translation exercise than developing and artfully writing a narrative patent (story).

Give us your idea, well take it from there.

You may be told, "Give us your idea, and we'll take it from there—just give us 'you're tired, your hungry, and your poor,' and we'll get you your pathway to patentship. We'll take your invention at the idea stage, or the embodiment at its release state, accepting the challenge of patenting it in, say, three months or less, before you violate the one-year rule and become your own prior art (this is the case of rushing a patent application to the altar as an afterthought on product 'completion' and field release). Oh, and please use this invention disclosure document, answering these five to ten questions, and we'll have at it."

You can and should retain your invention as a trade secret on your pathway, formulating a UCD during your product development life cycle based on your IP savvy understanding of the patent rubric. If you do, you will ensure a representation of a patentable invention that can be filed as a non-provisional application de-risked from fatal rejections within 1 year of public disclosure. With this approach you can and should file right the first time, and hopefully first (in patent strategy, there are considerations about filing as a provisional and flipping in one year).

Don't try this at home.

You may be told "just because you can, does not mean you should" applies to IP rights and their securement. With all things considered, I suggest the best way to protect and secure your claims is to work closely with an IP professional (most often an attorney), and not try to do it all yourself. Their reason is that there's a good bit of art, as well as a lot of skill in this gambit. Like it or not, yes, it's true that there is a bit of art and a lot of skill that goes with identifying and defining an IP asset, which is a crucial step in gaining

IP protection. Patents are extremely complicated documents. Even experienced patent attorneys can disagree on the best strategy, the best way to frame the details of the invention described, or the preferred claim language.

Try to think of IP-BC as a paint-by-numbers teaching tool. When a beautiful patent is drafted, it's not unlike a beautiful piece of art created by a master. At the same time, if the understanding of light, shadows, layers, and composition are explained with enough clarity and the brush and palate taken in hand, even a novice painter can create an equivalent look in a finished painting. That's a belief I hold close, and it is an underlying aspect of the UPL (see glossary) and the GP I teach as part of the pathway to patentship.

What many do not understand is that a good outcome relies as much on the client providing the right information the first time and at the right time, as it does on the attorney being good at what they do with that information. The process works best when the client is knowledgeable about what information the attorney needs and when they need it.

It's a fact that patent attorneys hate working with clients whose projects are a mess, especially if the client fails to timely provide the necessary information, and especially if the client does things in the dark to avoid a billable phone call. In these cases, the client will pay. They will probably not understand the invoices, and in the end be just plain unhappy. You can also be sure that in this kind of process, the client will not end up with what they wanted and will have lingering misgivings about whether the final product was done right.

More often than not, if the client has the Schwartz Method under their belt, the big-picture items will not be missed. The critical information for filing will be timely supplied because time was not spent fixing smaller stupid things that should never have become part of the exchange with counsel, and counsel will be engaged on only what matters most, allowing the client to avoid as many sleepless nights as their counsel might otherwise suffer.

10.3 During

On filing it's complicated to prepare the Doc Pak

You may be told not to try to prepare the filing packet. If you do not enjoy preparing and filing your own income taxes (without using a tax preparation software application), then you will not enjoy preparing and filing your own patent application. Let the IP professional and their staff do the work. It may not look like a lot when you see the final documents prepared and filed. However, it is not just the documents you are paying for, it is their expertise in knowing what to file when and how. For this reason, I share all of the proper forms and show you how to complete them correctly for filing with your particular patent application as a way to lower your stress levels—that part is not rocket science, and you can do it yourself if you are adventurous.

It's going to be expensive and take a long time.

You may be told: Look at these US Patent Office statistics for average time to obtain (2.2 years but more like 3 to 6), average cost to obtain ($48,000), typical duration (20 years from filing), and types of damages that are published, not to mention the costs if you file globally.

When were you ever average? In IP-BC I shift the burden of quality for the UCD and the steps to constructing all of the elements of the DOC PAK (what is filed as part of the application that puts the context of your application into play, especially the IDS), onto the innovation team. How I do that is in a series of levels that ensures all IP hunters are forewarned and forearmed about their role and task, so that there is zero impedance in getting the real invention, as P-E, popped out of the product development life cycle in as close to a non-provisional patent draft as possible. You're not average—it is possible. Do that, and you will be IP savvy, in the IP Zone as a team, and on the low end of the (dumb) bell shaped curve.

When to bring in IP counsel, and on what tasks? (Controlling tasking costs).

You may be told, bring your shift points to counsel at every turn without hesitation. If you don't, what you might think is a little fire may turn into a forest fire if allowed to smolder.

The real deal on this point is to not dismiss this point of view out of hand, but rather to see the light differently. A little fire is really insight into a critical change you may perceive as in a change to the P-E, or it may be a disclosure to a client that might trigger the 1 year rule, even if subject to a confidentiality agreement, and anywhere in between. From the point of view in IP-BC, the goal is to use the UPL and the GP to enable you to make clever choices about engaging counsel in your utility patenting workflow. If you know your process inside and out, you will intuitively know when to ask counsel for assistance. One key example is the timing, depth, and use of search. If an inventor starts their search too early, it will functionally fixate their inventive mojo. Counsel may be aware of the invention event and seek to get up to speed on the blue ocean, or the white spaces, maybe even the issues of enablement. But hold your horses. Search fits into the sequence of events in very impactful ways if implemented mindfully. In IP-BC, you will see that the first search is done by the innovator after they have their layman's claim and a definition of terms. Those searches are archived in preparation for a decision to patent or not to patent. A second deep dive search on the specific classification set will follow. Here, the choice of who will do it is crucial. In the Schwartz Method, you will continue this search in confidence using tools that may include a search team, or it may still be critical to keep it in house and secret. When the search is done by a patent drafter as part of the critical consideration for confirmation of enablement, that's a win. At the end of the day, the compilation of relevant search outcomes must be made in the form of an information disclosure document that is part of the filing package. Along with that must be a teachings explanation that preempts the potential use of any of that art against your claims for novelty and nonobviousness. That can still be drafted by the innovator's liaison without the use of out-of-pocket patent spending. IP SAVVY hunters are tuned into the timing for these considerations, and IP-BC shows you the decision points in its detailed four-step interval for the 30 Day IP Challenge. There will be other shift points in the journey, and choices about when to engage the patent spend. Controlling these choices, especially the ones during prosecution, will be the key to reducing your spending by up to 70 percent.

Representing yourself in front of the US Patent Office.

It is true that the US patent system is set up to allow inventors to represent themselves in the pursuit of a patent. You may be told that there are so many fatal preparation errors for the DIYer that doing this yourself may result in irreversible damage during prosecution. Whatever patent overhead a DIYer might expend will be fruitless, resulting in a final rejection and abandonment.

It is seductive to see what a patent counsel seeks with their invention disclosure forms, or one of the many web-based options offered a patent if you fill in the form. This positions them in the driver's seat. Don't be fooled by any of this since you can learn the patent rubric in IP-BC and timely create most of the critical contents yourself. If you do, if and when it's time to handle an interview with the examiner, you will be in the driver's seat and it will turn into a collaboration, allowing you a higher probability of prevailing with your claim(s).

You may be told that if you do take on the interview, it will raise a hornet's nest and it will not go well.

It may turn out that the best scenario is for you to appear with counsel, or if you do send counsel, only if they are proceeding with your guidance. First, you have a direct right to draft, file, prosecute, and represent yourself *pro se* (for yourself) in front of the US Patent and Trademark Office. However, in the thick of battle, it really does depend. The examiner is tasked with granting the inventor with an allowance, and in general examiners really do like and respect the owner of the IP. Their conflicting goal is to clear their desk of applications (for better or for worse), and this does drive what may emerge as cruelty in the prosecution phase. In truth, if the lead inventor has taken on the responsibility of understanding the patent rubric and the meaning behind the scope of their claimed monopoly, they are the best ones to argue over an objection. The best way to do that will emerge in the course levels. Just don't rule out the role of one of the inventive proponents in handling the examiner in the early impression step, when as surprising as this may sound, the examiner really doesn't understand your invention, and the last thing he or she can do is comprehend the scope of a claim that a patent counsel is driving as if it is obvious, an obvious right that the examiner is denying. That's a hornet's nest of its own making and will pit the examiner against counsel.

Lowest cost does not work when it comes to securing your IP.

To achieve the highest quality, lowest cost is not part of the consideration. It's going to cost you. In the IP-BC reality, you can do a lot of things to control costs, and I show you how and when to engage counsel on what the substantive issues really are. How much will it really cost to patent it?

You may be told that it's difficult to say. It depends on what the inventor provides with detailed (figures, descriptive explanations, etc.). Of course, there will be the unpredictable back and forth on a draft patent application between counsel and the inventor, as everyone grapples with describing relevant details. You may hear that there are ways to take simpler, lower-cost steps in the early stage of protection and leave the more complex, expensive steps for later. When you do go into the iterative sequence to reduce the reduction to practice to a competent patent draft, you may be told that the original estimate was low because you changed the target and increased the complexity. Basically, you might hear that if you knowingly withhold information about the complexity of your project, shame on you. It could result in a lowball estimate that becomes unrealistic when more of the details are revealed. This will result in lost interest in the project if you are not prepared to deal with the real, much more expensive cost, and you will risk not getting the best protection for your money. Since "we are in this business to make a profit, we can't work on razor-thin margins with risks of nonpayment when the going gets rough".

Fundamentally, when you do keep the iterative reductions of your invention going, you will be reducing the complexity of its patentable representation, but the key is doing that part yourself! Yes, you should try that at home. When you are told to give a description of the invention early, by answering a set of targeted questions to elicit the ah-ha feature and the minimal structure and function to make it so (before you really know the P-E and best mode yourself), then you are falling into the trap of what may really be an amorphous, even ambiguous invention disclosure with a very high-level description of your best guess of it. In this scenario, getting to the real invention along with drafting the reduction and minimizing the complexity will ensure this is the costliest process once the project is underway, because the number of back-and-forth iterations between you and your counsel will be unbearable. Further, now that we are in a first-to-file patenting world, the idea of the second mouse getting the cheese is really afoot.

Upending that notion is the key to your success. It is critical to get the simplest representation of your P-E and to do that first, with a claim that has suitable scope, but that may actually be the hardest thing to do first. It is something you should not defer, because by deferring the identity of the true invention, it's best mode, and a claim that will be infringed if others try to make, use, and/or sell it, could result in a door opener for all of your competition, rather than a door with your lock on it.

On your pathway to patentship: In no uncertain terms, the idea of keeping your invention as a trade secret until its patentable elements reveal themselves to you is fundamental to getting it right the first time as part of the product development life cycle. When you apply the iterative Schwartz Method before giving anything to patent counsel, you will be giving them a version of a UCD that anticipates the interdependencies in the patent rubric, the target of a patent drafting step, eliminating 75 percent of the back and forth. This is all explained in complete detail in IP-BC/ADVANCED and implemented in a dynamic document workflow sequence as part of ADVANCED-PRACTITIONER, where the UCD will be crafted using a proven engineering method for eliminating ambiguity and indefiniteness, the killers of SCA in applications drafted as bible patents..

10.4 After

Running up the steps.

When it comes to doing good work, operating efficiently, and keeping IP clients in the fold, you can find a good partner and they will do right by you. Everyone gets fulfillment when they can readily complete a project in the least amount of time and at the lowest cost, with the highest quality. Here's the rub. If you have it all done for you, and it's not right the first time, all of the costs in preparation will be tripled in prosecution, and the reason for those costs might entirely fall on an ill-conceived drafting process. This is compounded by the situation where a weak patent is allowed to publish. Once it's attacked, who's going to come to the rescue? Not ghost busters, I can assure you. It will likely be the counsel who drafted it or a department in the firm you retained that handles litigation. I have heard one too many times that the players on the field for you in this stage, if it does happen, are not only great at it, but that they run up the steps every morning with bells on their heels to pursue the offenders. From my perspective, you never want to get into this type of process, and the best way to avoid downstream risks with litigation is to get it right the first time, filed first, using IP-BC/the Schwartz Method. If you are faced with litigation, as I've pointed out in many places, let saner minds prevail first, take a deep breath, and see how the issues can be resolved in a mutual way.

11.0 General business considerations

11.1 Introduction to business considerations and the BBT

Business considerations are a big ocean of topics. Here, I try to sort out how and when they get intertwined with utility patenting. The first dimension on which the business considerations need to be considered is the how-to's of patenting operation behaviors. This set of issues represents the business aspects of being prepared and staying flexible during some of the steps, as you ride the bronco to the point of a gentle walk to the stable. The uneasy dynamic for patent-related business considerations is that they tend toward the unknowns and lead to probabilistic projections. This is a stark contrast to MPEP rules. In the big picture, you will find some of the business aspects are quid-quo-pro as in the general rule that if you want to raise money (e.g., promise and get investors interested in a ten-times return in three years), then you will need to have a patent pending and a business model to monetize it. This section sorts out some of the key angles in which business decisions tie in with and are intertwined with patenting.

Since this topic is multidimensional and intertwined, I use the before-during-after (B-D-A) approach to separate intervals out and to improve insights. A key guiding principle from IP-BC is what I call my big bang theory of IP capitalization (BBT) and it is a timeline perspective that turns on the critical event known as the notice of allowance (NOA). In BBT, I seek to start with the "as-if" NOA event T = 0 and walk the clock back in time reversing back to T = −5. For the business development cycle, I walk the clock forward from T=0 to T = +1 and so forth, in order to expose the monetary considerations, choices, and business risks along the commercialization pathway. When you integrate BBT into your thinking, you will be on your way to making the patent development process an integral part of your product development process. I linearized this to separate out the critical events. In real time, these steps are often interwoven, and the 1-year rule will come into dramatic relief.

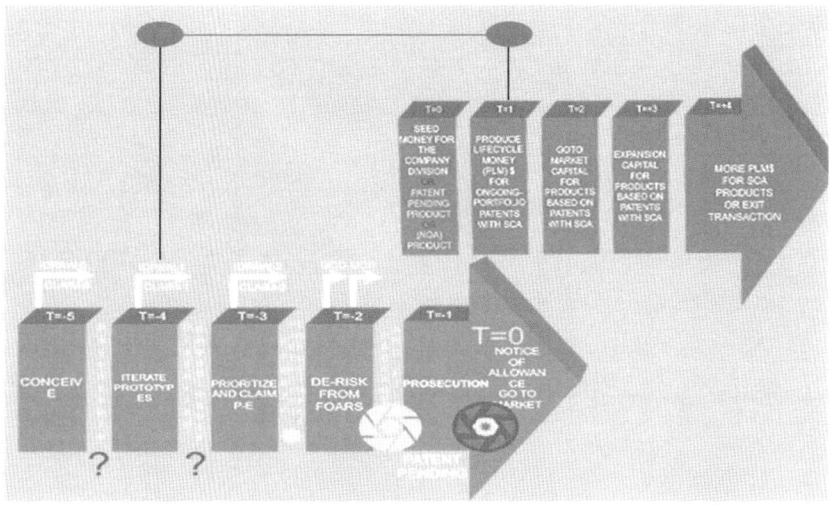

Fig 14. Big bang theory of IP capitalization

You will see that the type of business model you have will weigh heavily on the kind of patent decisions you make. A simple example here is the nature of patent objectives as an exclusively licensing-based business, versus a business that makes, sells, or uses a product. The scope of the claims you might seek would be broad, especially if your business goal was to license everyone for royalties nonexclusively. They would be narrower if you were solely focused on making your P-E.

In summary, I use BBT and the B-D-A framework along with identifying two categories.

(1)   The operational business considerations—in other words, how to get a patent and how to protect a patent once it's issued (mostly a before set of considerations) and

(2)   The monetization considerations, including establishing the value of the patent or patent portfolio and how to put a monopoly into practice—when the consideration is based on whether to make, use, and sell, or partner, license, or sell the patents.

As we go through this, trying to make crisp distinctions, there are grey areas in labeling and separating out the issues. You can readily understand that monetization considerations depend on both patent tactics and patent strategies. Try to make your own rules on how to keep patent tactics and strategies separated. You can formulate some of your own criteria, driven by your unique objectives about how to make your patent(s) work in the market. Some of the insights you use in making sense of the separation and timing of decisions will be easier to anticipate, and others will manifest or show themselves once you are in the fray. Stay open-minded and remain adaptive, as this kind of behavior will be the key to success. The following points should provide contrast and give you a framework for creating and interpreting your own business model along the various dimensions.

11.2 Before

Do you need patent counsel to get started and if so, what kind? The classification of "patent matter" is exceptionally well structured and identifies the many specialized areas for the purpose of separating art groups for filing. This level of complexity belies the simple truth that for the purpose of defining enablement and getting a properly scoped claim in the final filing, if you do retain a patent professional, they must be or have someone who is an expert in your area and has one or more sample patents they filed that you can look at. Use the Schwartz Method to evaluate their ability and see if they pass your filter for cost-effective final preparation. Generally, how much did their client pay and for what services, especially for prosecution?

Not all patent counsel are created equal either. There are certified patent attorneys, patent agents, and paralegals, all with different levels of skill and purpose when it comes to helping you prepare and prosecute a patent application.

Patent agents pass the registration examination and are listed with the US Patent Office. Taking this patent bar exam requires the individual seeking registration to formally apply, establish their moral character and reputation, cite their relevant qualifications, and argue for their competence in appearing before the patent office. So, if they are registered, their profile will be predetermined, and you can ask for this as part of your interview process. Remember that patent law is a federal legal process, and you will need to keep in mind that certain things that could happen along the pathway may also require legal advice in your state.

Patent agents can represent an inventor in front of the US Patent Office for the purpose of preparing, filing, and prosecuting patent applications, they are not authorized to offer legal advice. Even though MPEP is MPEP and that is the legal framework for all of this, there are limitations to patent agent's functional services after patents issue. They cannot represent you in a court on patent infringement or offer legal opinions relating to patent validity. If you know what you need when you need it (example-expertise on enablement), then you can benefit from their lower hourly billing rate. I said this before, when forming an engagement with a patent agent or patent counsel, it is my sense that it's better to be safe than sorry about confidentiality, especially if you use outside patenting experts. I advise that getting a confidentiality or nondisclosure agreement executed to protect your information is not something to be ashamed of when hiring any potential counsel since they talk to a lot of people in their inner circles and it's really your trade secrets in play. Also, when forming the engagement letter, it makes sense to not permit the firm to market your name as a client for obvious competitive reasons, unless they're big guns and you want to strike fear into the hearts of potential competitors. Another aspect here is how to structure the engagement and center it on only substantive issues. At the end of the day, the billing rates are the billing rates, and you're going to have to bite the bullet, but make sure it's only on work you preauthorized, reserving the opportunity to look at any situation or issue first and before any investigative work is performed.

A patent attorney has all the credentials for practicing at the US Patent Office as a patent agent as well as having a law degree from an accredited law school and at least one state bar certification. So, you will likely want to know which state your potential attorney can practice in, especially if you are dealing with injunctions or with declarative judgments. Additionally, any lawyer who received a law degree and passed a state bar exam is qualified to not only give you patent legal advice but could also be a valuable resource on business law issues.

The clinches of working with patent counsel.

Since I am only covering utility patents and not the other forms of IP, if you are going down multiple paths to protect your IP including trademarks and design patents, you will want to think through how many skills your counsel possesses or whether you will need a team of legal resources.

In principle, you have trade secrets across a spectrum of patent actions and business considerations. The intimate nature in which the patent and business issues are tied together is yours and your cohorts. If you have patent assistance on your team because your company has patent counsel, then you are in luck because all of the employees are bound to the same degree of confidentiality and trade secrets will be maintained and defended using company policies.

If you are using outside counsel, deciding how and when to share your business goals and objectives is a much bigger issue. Can outside counsel really help you with your game plan outside of the patent effort? Do you need them to help you with license agreements or with partnership agreements? What's to say that if you terminate your arrangement for any one of a number of reasons, that your training them on your profile and parameters for operating won't come back and bite you downstream when they are working with others? There are no exclusives with outside firms. You will pay up front with a retainer, you will get billed day by day for services rendered, and you will pay everything you owe them if you terminate with a bill that might somehow have gotten rung up, as in all of the overseas agent fees that they might have paid through their affiliated agents, which you authorized, that come due later. When a bill for final services rendered appears to the tune of $35,000 or $75,000, rest assured you will be forced to pay it.

When looking for the perfect legal partner, be resourceful. Network, use your intuition, and do research. Look at patents issued in your field and who represented those clients. In reality, that is what your competitors are doing, so again, I am cautious in suggesting that you find a strategic legal partner. It is possible to structure the engagement to make the deal worthwhile for everyone, while having them look and feel like in-house counsel. No one can tell you how to do this, and I assure you this is much more of a slippery slope. If you have mastered the Schwartz Method and the counsel you are working with has taken IP-BC and is certified in using the Schwartz Method, you can be sure that you are going to get what you ask for, you are going to get what you pay for, you will understand your bills, and you will be mindful in defining substantive work.

11.3 During

If you are retaining patent counsel and you have to pay for it, you will be in for some interesting discoveries. Expect to pay no less than $250 an hour, but don't be surprised to find that a senior partner on your case might bill at $1,200 per hour. Clearly, the tag-team framework will determine the effective billing rate, but you can expect it to be on average in the range of $500 per hour. With that said, the nature of the work will determine who is on the task at the firm, and if it's a paralegal, then you will see that work as administrative and billed at a suitable fee.

Don't expect to have your patent counsel buy into your initiative and make special arrangements for fees. There are circumstances with venture capital engagements that can be used to limit initial patent expenditures. That might work, but this is beyond the scope of this book. Patent firms are for-profit entities, and they will have their fees before, during, and after, so the idea of DIAAY with IP-BC and the Schwartz Method is to minimize these fees while maximizing your asset value. I have pointed out how to get patents to issue with SCA. If you use my UPL and GP, you can manage this balancing act and it can be win-win.

How to predict what you will spend with outside counsel.

Only you will be able to assess the true complexity of your product or idea. In principle, if you follow the UPL and GP, at the end of your product development cycle, you will have a UCD that represents it with MPEP-compliant features. When it comes to converting that document into a draft of a patent application, the process will be more akin to cutting and pasting in a translation, where the patent is generated by a straightforward editing process.

It is true that getting to a quiesced UCD is going to take time and effort. If you DIAAY, then the cost will factor into your overhead and not be paid out in billable fees. You will hear that estimating exactly how long it will take to complete the patent is unanswerable because the complexity is unpredictable. When there are changes to be made, you will have to go back to square zero and start over to avoid risks of fatals. If the act of final preparation is deferred until the IDPAW is quiesced, then you're going to get what you pay for and ensure that the quality is built in and that you understand the legal claims and their scope when you get the application back for final review. If you invest on order of one hour per week on your ID-PAW during product engineering, then the actual act of translation involving preparation and filing could take on average only sixteen hours (two business days).

Under any other process—that is, with the invention disclosure document provided early to a charging agency such as patent counsel, many more factors will contribute to the billable expenses, not limited to complexity. Even more so, the lack of depth and organization of the information provided in the invention disclosure document. You will form a black hole and end up with even more conversations with counsel, and this could turn into big bucks, depending on how responsive you are and whether or not you are rushing at the US Patent Office. It is highly unlikely that a utility patenting project will get a flat fee. Also, just know that if you do use the Schwartz Method as your core process, then if you discover that you will need to make multiple filings for a related set inventions in your discontinuity, you may be able to flatten out the preparation and conversion costs for the subsequent applications and file mostly at the cost of patent office fees. By doing this, you can identify the tasks outside counsel will be asked to do, along with tamping down the retainer they will ask for. Most likely, they will be seeking on order of 50 percent of what their internal estimate of the work will cost up front. You can self-manage your way to a much better engagement with counsel if you use the Schwartz Method to organize upfront before reaching out for this step in the process.

Picking a patent professional to help you.

Obviously, if you listen to the Morgan and Morgan commercials for selecting legal service partners, you wouldn't go to a dentist if you need arm surgery (they like to make it scarier and use heart valve surgery). It makes sense to start your search early, while you are developing your UCD, so that you have choices and can get a contrasting sense of who is really going to come through for you. When you know what you're trying to patent, your ability to sort out the right attorney will be a simple step and you will not get going with the wrong player. It will be important to know who will be the "stuckee" in the eventual workflow for the engagement. Read that the low-level patent personnel used. You will need to identify the senior partner who will likely be the one closing you on the engagement. Knowing the technical backgrounds of their team will be one of the most critical factors because the real issue in getting an SCA patent is how well you support your P-E with enablement that meets the threshold for MPEP compliance. Look at other patents they have filed in your area. If you're in pharmaceuticals, the skill sets of the patent players will include chemistry and biology, while for mechanicals like consumer products or robotics, they will be electrical and mechanical engineers. This is all kind of obvious if you know what you're doing up front.

Remember that when the firm proposes combining one of their experienced people with an associate, it could be a good thing. At the same time, if you know what type of substantive work you are seeking for any billing event, you can see whether you need fifteen minutes from the senior for a strategy chat on claim scope or whether they put two hours of senior time into the invoice. If you use the Schwartz Method to do most of the work to transform your invention into the layman's Claim #1 and its Figure #1, you will minimize all of the potential outlays for the conversion to a patent draft. Just be wary if you see more than 25 percent of the billing generated by a senior partner, because that is the sign you turned your invention over too early.

When it comes to other related legal services like licensing or litigation, you will need to sort out the potential resource using different criteria. In licensing, get a sample license agreement in your classification-of-matter area (your technology). Are they also litigators? Be careful. Litigators may be more aggressive by nature or less inclined to negotiate resolutions before court processes unfold.

When you are in prosecution, there will be other issues to face, and you need to make sure that you get the first right of review on any action that could involve a substantive response (vs. a technicality). These actions have time limits as well, so knowing that the firm is capable of and willing to give you a commitment on timely support can play a role in your decision.

If you do decide to use a larger firm instead of a solo practitioner, you will be faced with an additional set of business issues. The Blue Cross Blue Shield commercial where they have the client in a testimonial saying "it feels like I'm your only client" is a great one as it conveys the idea that you can contract with the biggest and the best but receive services as if given by a solo practitioner who has only you as the client. Here again, you will be able to sort out who to trust and when, if you know what you need up front. Forewarned is forearmed in this selection consideration, even more so than in some of the others. If you go to a larger firm, you will need to be persistent in order to not get lost, pay your bills on time without asking any questions, and keep the project exciting because they're human too. If it looks like you're about to go off a cliff, they will be just as likely to put the blame back on you rather than take responsibility and risk litigation. You will be the one that keeps them on your pathway to patentship—you are steering the ship under the Schwartz Method business approach, and if you can navigate to your destination, it's because you knew where you were going in the first place.

As in any team effort, the skill sets of the individual cohorts will be very different as will their experience. Since I'm focused solely on utility patenting, it goes without saying that if you are picking any outside resource, you don't want it to be their first rodeo. If you will need someone to do hard core drafting revisions on your final iteration of the IDPAW, it's worth checking if they also have the business or strategy skills to help you with big picture issues, but so what? If they don't, no worries. If you know where you're going, you can find other helpers along the way. The key is to keep your inventive stuff a trade secret as long as possible along with your business and patent strategy. Your commercial model is even more important to keep confidential when you're partnering, licensing, or litigating.

As an individual inventor, emerging startup, you can anticipate that you will probably be at a disadvantage working with big law. Just go back to the BCBS commercial message and ask yourself if that's really possible. If you have an uncle in the big firm that's practicing in your area and taking you on, then you'll probably be fine. With the larger firms, you will pay more because that's their business model with their brand named clients. If on the other hand you are fortunate enough to find the right specialty patent firm, if you need one, you may be in a better position to get favorable engagement terms and better support.

Most business transactions that are billable will be done with email and PDFs, so it won't matter where the patent resource you pick lives. This is a new feature that is dis-intermediating the delivery of legal services, and the competition for providing patent assistance is probably at the highest level it's been in decades. This bodes well for negating favorable costs in your actual engagements when needed.

At the end of the day, it's really your responsibility to know the critical parameters for the success of your business, and what would end it all if found out by a competitor who could actually do something with or about it. Knowing this will help guide you on the pathway from the trade secret stage to how you will draft, the type of patent you will file, and the type of prosecution you will experience.

If push comes to shove and you find out that you can't patent your invention, it's better to do this early and in total control of the framework. If you can compete without patent protection because of some unique competitive advantage you have other than IP, then you will know that and you will take an exit ramp off the pathway to patentship. The way you might manage your business under these circumstance is the province of other business consultants and professional partners who can assist you with a unique value proposition and an operational strategy. Passion is the determinant here, as inspiration can provide more success than perspiration alone, even without a patent.

Since your issued patent will cover the technology innovation in your products, it will be part of your go-to market game plan and serve as one of the best ways to deter a competitor. At the same time, if you have a weak patent and a competitor can offer an equivalent product without infringing, your patent may just not do the trick for you. At the same time, it may allow more than one player to help create an even bigger market. If you can keep your patent validity without being to enforce your patent in court, that's what I call a happy DIAAY. Just know, if you think you have to send a cease and desist letter, be careful because you could initiate a countersuit and a declarative judgment in the state that your competitor is operating. Ugly.

When working with outside patent resources, you will pay for everything—not only the filing and prosecution fees. You will be out of pocket for all of these costs so that you can't say you won't pay at any time along the way. If you don't pay, your patent company can and will place a lien on your assets, and should you try to get liquidity, you will have to get the lien removed. Don't start with outsiders unless you know you can pay your way to the finish line.

11.4 After

If you planned ahead and had a supporting business model to leverage your IP, then you will be in a position to utilize cash flow to further fund your efforts. If your potential gains appear to warrant ten times return for investors in three years (or so), then you can leverage your IP for additional investments to scale the business. These are the time intervals in BBT that follow $T = 0$ (notice of allowance and also market entry).

In the end will my patent have value?

Patent assets are difficult to assign value. You will also need to consult a tax professional because how you represent them on your balance sheet can determine if you live or die. If you can establish a value and position them as depreciable, you can help with cash flow. On the other hand, if you can defer their valuation and claim all of your out-of-pocket spending as expenses, you may be able to show losses during the development phases. As an LLC, you can carry losses to your personal tax returns, and this could play into your business plans. All of this is really beyond the scope of this book.

The first step in the effort to assign any values is to get a patent pending or issued. Patents are assets, and you must account for them, period. Also keep in mind the idea of the seven hundred-pound gorilla and the notion of having a portfolio of patents. This will result in multiple dimensions for valuation, driven by the business model for the combination. Playing these cards right could result in the poker pot doubling or even tripling in the amount along with your probability of garnering potential returns for you, your family, and your investors.

Run the numbers and know that if you kept your patent spend under $25,000, saving potentially 70 percent or more on what you would have otherwise spent if you didn't use the Schwartz Method, and you could establish a valuation of more than $1 million based on forecasted licensing revenue or product sales, you will have repositioned your company to become a serious contender in your market. If you don't patent, you won't be able to do this kind of math.

At the end of the day, if you don't ostensibly take the steps to put utility patents into play as barriers to competition, then your competitors will race you in the market by copying your expensive R&D and they will be able to compete at a lower cost. Watch your market share dwindle if this scenario plays out.

With a patent as kingmaker, you can get more creative over time in generating innovative revenue streams. As you get into turning your patents into a business, you will manifest many new ways to make money that you may not have thought of on day one.

In one of many examples, with a patent, you will be able to identify other companies using technology covered by your patents. If one or more of these companies are not direct competitors, they may be potential partners with the right business contract. Channels might open up where the total available market can be expanded as a result. Investors love this.

In some cases, as shown in my IP Zone chart, your work might attract one or more government agencies. Hundreds of millions of dollars in grant money are available to fund critical research that relates to your core innovations and the interests of your key IP hunt cohorts. When you apply for a grant and get your invention work to be government funded, you will most likely be giving the funding body in the government rights to the funded invention with the concomitant right to practice your invention. If you can see ways to use your invention in parallel, then all will go well. Each case will bear specific scrutiny.

Your future as an IP SAVVY.

When you get to the starting gate, you will not only have your patent but a business plan for monetizing your innovation. You will have made crucial decisions about the type of patent you developed, including its focus on a single invention first. You will have tightened up your application, so if you file globally, you will be tied into translations with the least cost and the most clout. You will have identified partners to help you build your market and you will be off to the races with the holy grail, patent grant in hand. You will have a patent that has a clean file wrapper because you de-risked it from FOARs before filing. The patent will be seen as having SCA because it was filed first, was right the first time, had claims scoped to your P-E, and included a detailed description of enablement in your field of art that allowed another to practice it without experimentation. You will be operating in patent eligibility areas with compete novelty and your invention will be cited as unobvious because you submitted an airtight IDS, which lists all the patents you patent over, including potential competitors.

APPENDIX – The Schwartz Method revealed

The entire Part 2 of this book hinges on your understanding of the Schwartz Method. This appendix seeks to share the details of the method at a sufficient level for you to not only grasp how it works but also see why it is the key method for de-risking your patent draft from fatal office action rejections before filing. As much as I try, teaching this is a dialectical challenge, and in this sense, you will want to use the GLOSSARY that follows with the functional description in this section. Don't be frustrated with the acronyms but rather embrace them as they are the keys to reframing all of your conversations about how to acquire a great utility patent.

There are numerous references to the course Intellectual Property BoostCamp (IP-BC) throughout the explanations. As much as it is my goal to get you IP SAVVY with just this book, the more adventurous hunters will want to opt in for the course level that is most closely tied to their utility patenting role and title. When and if you do, you will augment your understanding and retention. You will find opportunities to apply the UPL and GP with your own inventive matter and formulate your own patent drafts that are airtight and right the first time.

No matter which content you use, you will be ahead of the game changing conversations on how to convert your idea into a patent application. Let TSM show you the way.

Detailed description of the Schwartz Method and how it works.

TSM is based on the fundamental GP that "what you see is not how you get" (WYSINHYG). To explain how this works, a simple graphical image that depicts how the MPEP order in which a patent is delivered is interwoven with the Schwartz rubric and how a TSM patent draft is created. In the following figure, you will see that the numeric sequence depicts the ordered set of MPEP rule 111/113 compliant patent application sections, while the alphanumeric letters, in alphabetic sequence, show the order in which the critical elements are created.

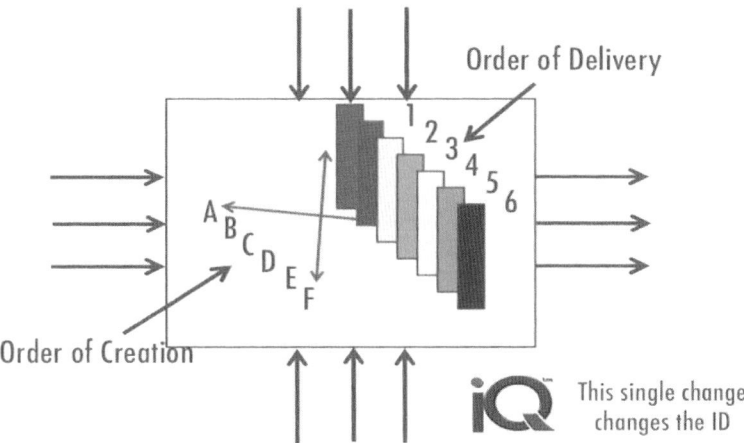

Fig 15. MPEP order of delivery with respect to TSM order of creation

Now that you have this GP rule, you will see how each of the templates is used to iteratively elicit critical entries into the invention disclosure patent application workbook (IDPAW), that will incrementally compile and automatically translate into a utility compliant disclosure (UCD) and finally into a utility compliant patent application (UCPA). In this figure, the dialectical completion of these data records is made during the product development cycle as the elements quiesce, and the entries stabilize and lock in on the P-E.

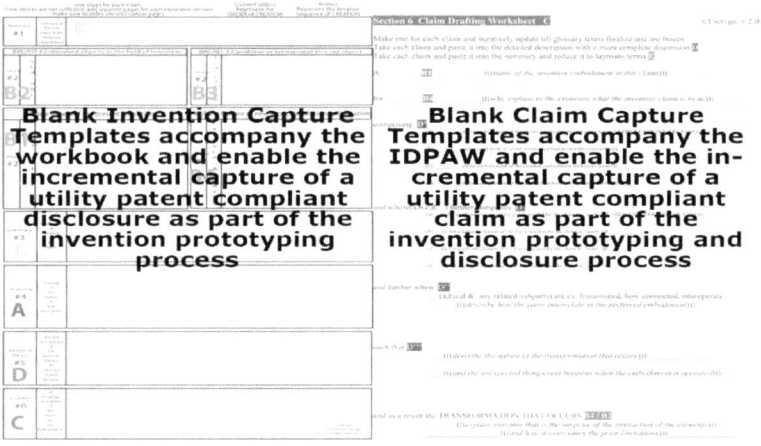

Fig 16. TSM template elements iteratively used to comprise a utility compliant patent draft

The following sequence of steps show the complete TSM loop when forming a utility compliant patent application (UCPA). I use a set of descriptive graphical icons to reveal the secret sauce behind TSM. If you have another method to do this, then use it in good stead. If you find this method is the one you prefer, then adopt it for all of your patent drafting. The best way to do this is to opt in for the ADVANCED level using the coupon provided. There you will be able to access and download the reusable PDF's for each of these templates. If you have a drafting project underway, it may make sense to upgrade to ADVANCED-PRACTITIONER where a complete set of dynamic .docs are provided, along with a 4 interval sequence that walks you thru the TSM sequence, step by step, with your own inventive matter. This level is called the 30 day DIY challenge and is designed to get you to a UCPA within 4 weeks or less. The first figure below depicts the multi-stage iteration of the Schwartz Method (TSM) using the invention disclosure patent application workbook entries (IDPAW). The subsequent figures show how the method is developed into an MPEP compliant patent application. There is sufficient detail here to enable you to own and use TSM. If you want to scale this with your team, it is recommended that you use the IP-BC course to gain access to the reusable templates along with step-by-step instruction on how to apply them.

Fig. 17 TSM sequence (a,b,c,d,e,f,g)

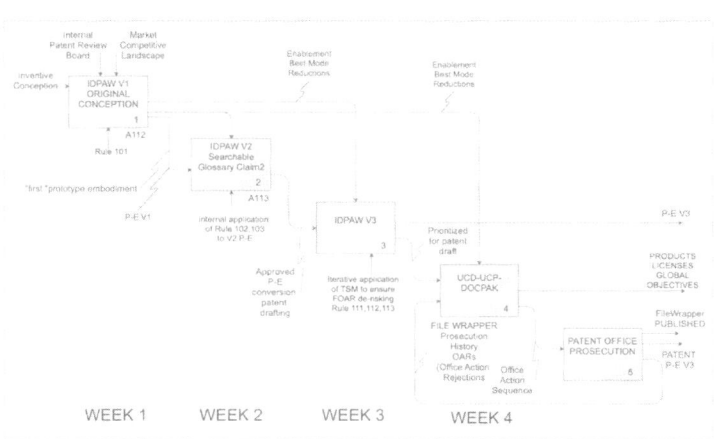

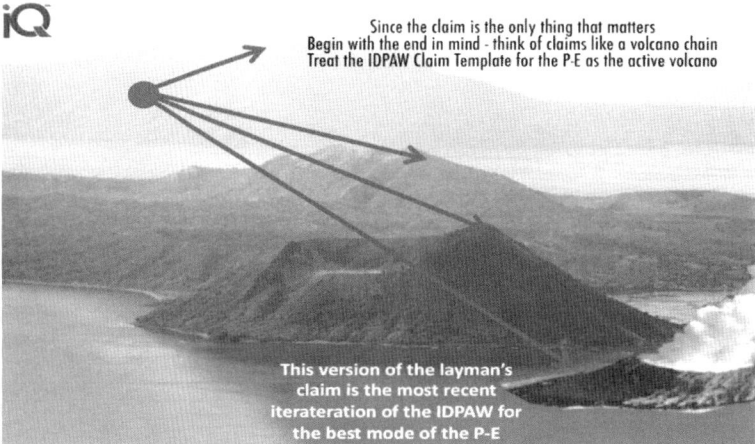

The TSM engineering approach places
the elements of the P-E into the claim
template. Section C is the UPL grammar.

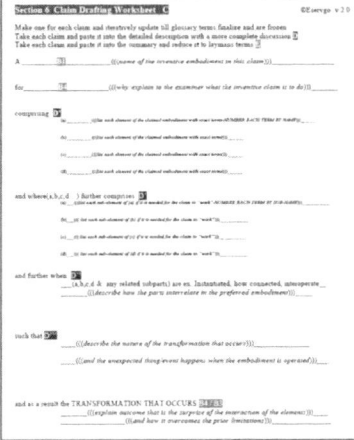

The IDPAW and the claim template are dialectically created
"at the same time" much like "the chicken and egg"

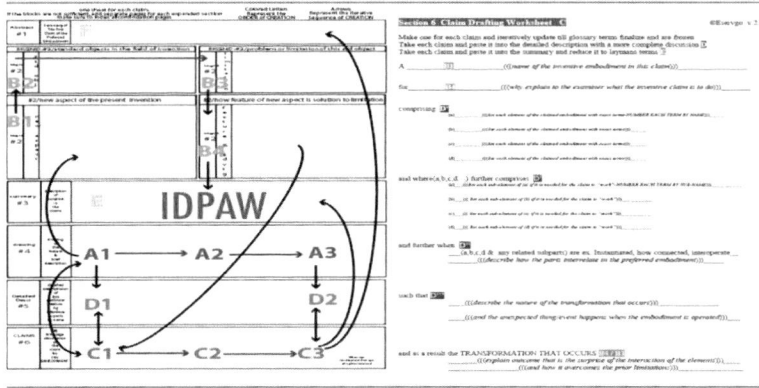

During creation you just iterate on
A1-C1-D1 / A2-C2-D2 / A3-C3-D3

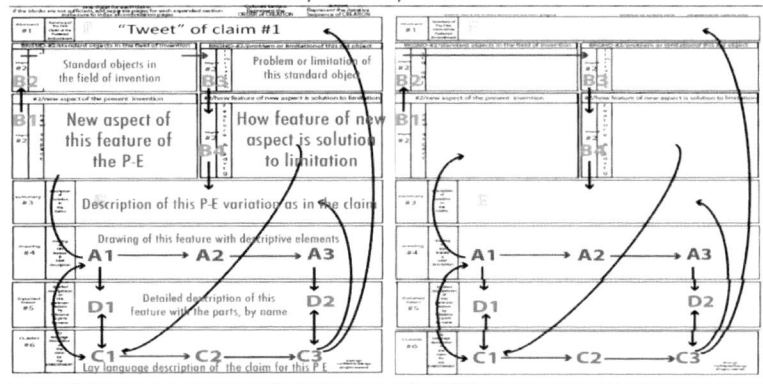

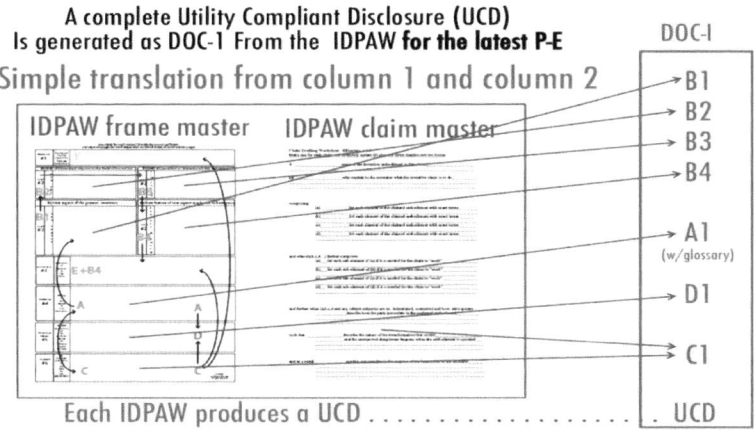

A complete Utility Compliant Disclosure (UCD)
Is generated as DOC-1 From the IDPAW for the latest P-E

Simple translation from column 1 and column 2

IDPAW frame master   IDPAW claim master

DOC-I

B1
B2
B3
B4

A1
(w/glossary)

D1

C1

Each IDPAW produces a UCD . . . . UCD

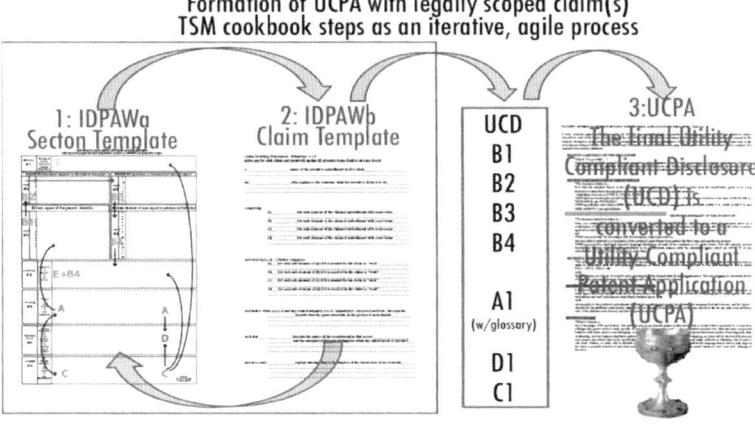

Formation of UCPA with legally scoped claim(s)
TSM cookbook steps as an iterative, agile process

1: IDPAWa
Secton Template

2: IDPAWb
Claim Template

UCD
B1
B2
B3
B4

A1
(w/glossary)

D1
C1

3:UCPA

The final Utility
Compliant Disclosure
(UCD) is
converted to a
Utility Compliant
Patent Application
(UCPA)

In summary, the purpose of this graphical description is to enable you to get your arms around how the TSM method works so you can form your own understanding of this tried, true, and proven patent engineering process. Understanding this will facilitate changing every one of your utility patenting conversations, since applying TSM will drive every aspect of your utility patent drafting. This description of TSM is complete enough for you to take it away and integrate your own big bang sequence of utility patent capture with your product development lifecycle. If you want to accelerate even more quickly down the utility patenting corridor of uncertainty, then make the most use of TSM. Use IP-BC with this book to get you and your team IP SAVVY. When you do proceed, you can use the IP SAVVYS learning management system at https://www.ipboostcamp.com to explore the entire framework including all of the levels and how to assign them to your cohort team based on their utility patenting role and tasking.

What follows here are expanded versions of the templates that comprise the Schwartz Method. When you use my time lapsed flow in 4 intervals, which I show, measured in weeks, as week1-week4, included as part of the 30 day do-it yourself challenge, each of the progressive iterations of these forms for your P-E will result in a utility compliant patent application.

The purpose of providing the expanded forms here is to ensure you can clearly see the terms in the TSM UPL and follow the arrows of the GP as the method for patent formation. There is no getting away from the complexity of drafting. However, by showing you a way you can implement your drafting as an iterative engineering process following the steps in order, should give you comfort and hope that you can implement this within your own patent development project.

I want to re-emphasize that these templates replace any Invention Disclosure Document, typically asked for by patent counsel. Again, I repeat myself. In order to become proficient in drafting DIAAY using my method, I recommend using the coupon code at the end of the book and opting in to take the IP-BC/ADVANCED course level. Once in ADVANCED, you can upgrade to ADVANCED-PRACTITIONER and extend your time interval for using the dynamic document files while preparing a UCD with your own inventive matter.

The templates following are the claim section (Section C, Section 6), the invention disclosure patent application workbook (IDPAW) entry, and the utility compliant disclosure (UCD). After finishing a UCD you will generate a utility compliant patent application (UCPA). The step for doing this is taught in the recommended course level above.

Claim drafting worksheet : Section C of TSM/Section 6 of MPEP formatted patent draft

A (B1(name of the inventive embodiment in this claim)

x

_____

for B4(why: explain to the examiner what the inventive claim is to do)

x

_____

comprising D'
(list each element of the claimed embodiment with exact terms-NUMBER EACH TERM BY NAME)
   (a)
   (b)
   (c)

and where(a,b,c...) further comprises D

(list each sub-element if it is needed for the claim to "work"-NUM-
BER EACH TERM BY SUB-NAME)

    (a)

    (b)

    (c)

and further when D"

(a,b,c & any related subparts) are ex. Instantiated, how connected,
interoperate

(((describe how the parts interrelate in the preferred embodiment)))

x

---

such that D"'

((((describe the nature of the transformation that occurs)))

(((and the unexpected thing/event happens when the embodiment
is operated)))

x

---

and as a result, the TRANSFORMATION THAT OCCURS B4 / B3

(((explain outcome that is the surprise of the interaction of the elements)))

(((and how it overcomes the prior limitations)))

x

IDPAW

Title of invention:

x _____

Name of lead inventor:

x _____

Date: / /

Revision #: _____

Name of author_____

Initials:_____

Date:_____

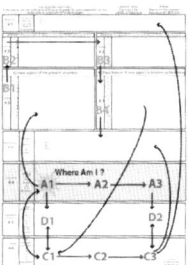

Create Section A: Drawing(s) of P-E

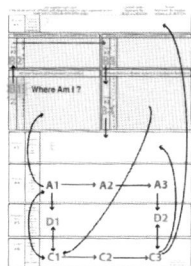

Create Section B: B1-B2-B3-B4

For the DRAWING/SKETCH of the Innovative Invention P-E answer the following(insert text):

B1: New Aspect of the Present Invention

B2: Standard Objects in the Field of Invention

B3: Problems and Limitations of the Standard Objects

B4: How the New Aspect of the Present Invention is a Solution to the Limitations of B3

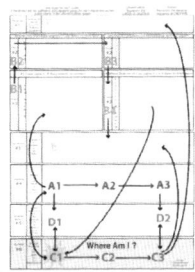

Create Section C: C1 (and derivatives)

Use the CLAIM TEMPLATE(ref claim drafting worksheet C)
as the guide to writing a LAYMAN's version of Claim 1 for your P-E:

Name(s) of inventors that contributed to this element and representation of the P-E (note: these
entries will be the named inventors in the filing papers and will need to comply with all filing docs):

Name:_____

Name:_____

Name:_____

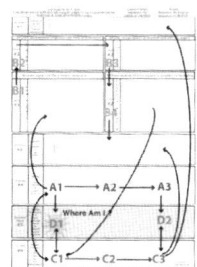

Create Section D: D1 (and derivatives)

After numbering and naming each essential element of the DRAWING of the P-E in Section A, CREATE A GLOSSARY, then copy and paste the LAYMAN's CLAIM from the claim template in Section C and EDIT that description by placing the names (identical for antecedent reference) and the number for each (this is a European STANDARD and worth following for both completeness and compliance if filing internationally). Add any other descriptive matter that will tie together the inventive matter in a way that not only the EXAMINER, but any other beneficiary of your work will be able to read and understand:

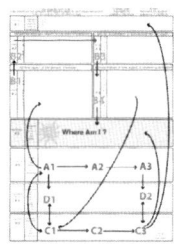

Create Section E: Description of this variation in the CLAIM

When your initial claim of the PE, the drawing of it, the glossary, and the terms for labeling all the numbered elements have quiesced for this P-E, make a copy of the CLAIM here, remove all the said's, and wherefores, and so forth to create a simple summary of this claim-just like the label for this section of the IDPAW UCD MPEP compliant document says (p.s. you can decide NOT to complete this part yet and WAIT. It can be done when all the IDPAW P-E sets are combined into a complete UCD(utility compliant disclosure):

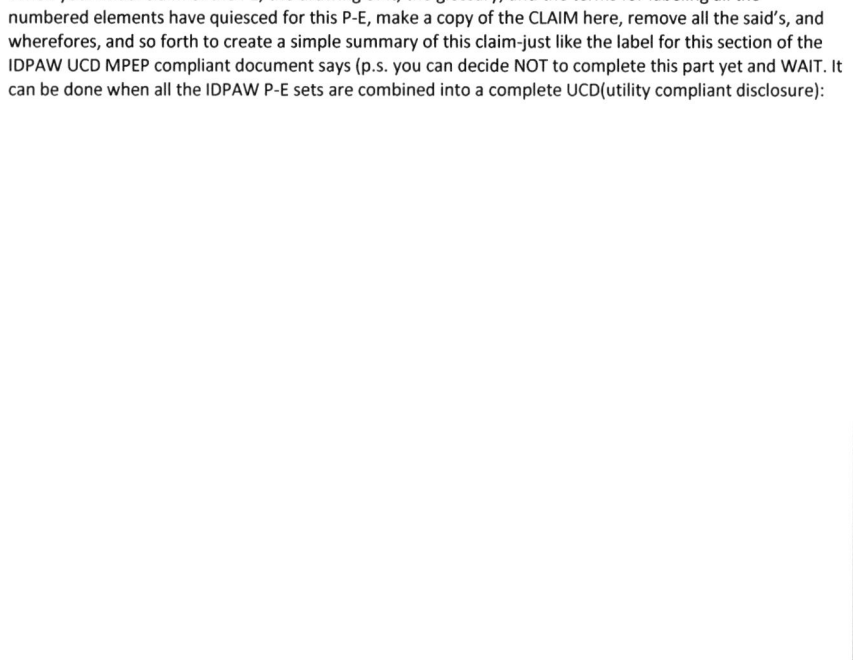

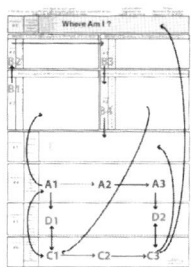

Create Section F: A SIMPLE summary of the first CLAIM of the P-E

In this VERY LAST step, one you can delay until all of the variations of the P-E's have been represented and vetted using the IDPAW worksheet template pages, make a super summary for any 3rd grader to read of what your invention is. USE the final iteration of CLAIM #1. Take it, copy it and paste it here. Use the Section B1 and B4 to both set the context for where your invention fits and how you overcome limitations in the field of standard objects in this classification of this invention, i.e., your bold summary of how you define over the prior art. If you can do this, the EXAMINER will make a substantially more constructive evaluation of your application in his first Office Action on the merits of your claimed innovation.

Create Section TITLE: proposed name(s) of this invention
(use the preferred name for this revision on the first page of this IDPAW)

Name:_____

_____

_____

Alternate Name:

_____

_____

You have completed an IDPAW description of the P-E of your invention.

Since you did this following the ORDER OF CREATION A-B-C-D-E-F, you have what will be a disclosure that will meet the rule 101,102,103, and 112 requirements.

If you want to GENERATE a NON-PROVISIONAL patent application, the next step is to take each of these ALPHANUMERIC sections (A-F) and paste them into the UCD document which holds the SEQUENCE of DELIVERY (Sections 1-6). When you are quiesced, then translate the UCD into a UCPA by using the transitional text and converting the layman's claim into a properly scoped legal claim. In this way, have a complete non-provisional patent application by completing each Section(1-6). You may decide to file this version of your patent application draft as a provisional. Refer to the IP SAVVYS book and review the 1-year rule to decide if this is the way to go.

The TSM documents formed at each stage of your product development effort can be read and understood if the cohorts on the inventive team are familiar with using TSM. Most importantly, the key conversation with the Patent Counsel you are using to make a final analysis and editing revision before filing should be based on the final delivery of the TSM papers and not an invention disclosure document.

Reminder that for rules 111/113, detailing EVERYTHING that must accompany a filing, like the chain of invention, Information Disclosure Document, assignment affidavits and so forth, is required when forming your DOC PAK for filing. I include the package of USPTO forms for what that "looks like" in the download reference file of ADVANCED. On filing, your IP liaison will need to complete and file all of those papers for your application to be accepted into the art groups queue for examination. Avoid any technical rejection for improper filing and you will guarantee your date of submission. If you did make any technical error in the set of papers, then subject to your timely correction of those technical errors, you will preserve your filing date. Any rejection for missing or incorrect elements of the 111/113 package are easy to fix and must be fixed within the specified time of that OA rejection, typically 30 days. Shame on any rejection for those technicalities, yet they do happen, and without finger pointing, just fix them without hesitation so you can get into the queue for examination on merits.

UCD

(Utility Compliant Disclosure)

Title of invention:
_____
X _____

Name of lead inventor:
X _____

Date: / /

Revision #: _____

Name of author_____

Initials:_____

Date:

A truly complete patent application contains all of these elements, although it is possible to file and get a patent allowed that minimizes certain elements in each of the below subject areas, at the end of the day, what ends up mattering is solely the CLAIMS and their antecedent support in the detailed description of the drawings, i.e. The detailed description of the invention-and it HAS TO WORK in accordance with at least each of the embodiments featured for the claims to be allowed. Validity is a matter that comes into play once a patent is actually issued and will be a subject of a separate best practices statement. In order to generate a UCD, take the sections of the IDPAW and paste them into the sequentially numbered and named sections of a patent that follow here:

SECTION 1-ABSTRACT OF THE DISCLOSURE – ORDER CODE <<F>>
"Object Y is provided....."
This paragraph provides a simple language description of the operation of the CLAIM representing the preferred embodiment. Therefore, it is essential that the inventive feature of the innovation be known and clearly articulated, and that the graphic representation of that embodiment be carefully selected for the "first or Fig 1 of the application, and that the general language here depict that in layman's terms.

SECTION 2-BACKGROUND OF THE INVENTION – ORDER CODE <<B>>

"This invention relates to.....

First state the standard objects in the invention by either quoting out the descriptive matter from the classification guide or by using descriptive matter from relevant prior art from the field and subfield of this specific invention-

>state these elements as TYPE A, TYPE B, TYPE C

THEN-discuss current prior art and known public solutions stating the limitations of those known solutions in the form of PROBLEM A, PROBLEM B, and PROBLEM C

THEN-specifically state what is NEW in this invention by saying which new aspects such as NEW ASPECT A, NEW ASPECT B, and NEW ASPECT C new and different

SECTION 3-SUMMARY OF THE INVENTION – ORDER CODE <<E>>

"The invention therefore relates to....

Here, you restate NEW ASPECT A, NEW ASPECT B, and NEW ASPECT C in effect repeating what you indicated above as a continuation of the representation of the proposed innovation that is patentable, and then briefly describe the FEATURE of the inventive application that is associated with the new aspect of the invention that solves the problem for each of problems A,B,& C.

and

THEN you must state "In accordance with the invention, what is provided is...

and here what is required is a description of the preferred embodiment that matches the first claim and matches the abstract

THEN you provide a functional layman's language description of each of the variations in all of the claims. This will naturally include descriptions of each of the embodiments(likely to be independent claims) AND the dependent claims which are ASPECTS of any embodiment.... VARIATION 1,2,3,4,5 as in each claim.

SECTION 4- BRIEF DESCRIPTION OF DRAWINGS – ORDER CODE <<A>>

"The above and other objects and advantages of the invention will be apparent from consideration of the following detailed description, taken to conjunction with the accompanying drawings, in which like reference characters refer to like parts throughout, and in which FIG.1....FIG.2....FIG.3....etc
AND
for each figure, provide an ID number and a description of the element that ID number references. This not only ensures consistent choice of language, but it also ensures that every element that has a # is actually named by reference.

SECTION 5- DETAIL DESCRIPTION OF INVENTION-ORDER CODE <<D>>

A Preferred embodiment (FIG 1-n) described in detail by referencing each of the numbers. This section should have a description of every figure and every element from the ID number list in Section 4. Nothing can be left out. Everything has to hang together for each embodiment and each embodiment when finally detailed has to work

AND

subsequently to the preferred embodiment detailed above which is to match the abstract, the summary first embodiment, and the figure 1 selected for the preferred embodiment, then you are to describe in sufficient detail so that one skilled in the art can make your invention each of the alternate embodiments and their respective aspects.

SECTION 6-CLAIMS – ORDER CODE <<C>>

"What is claimed is.....

this is the magic of the application. The patent is only as good as the claims in this section and no product that is marketed by a competitor infringes this patent unless it reads directly on one of the claims in this section. Any competitive product that offers the same unexpected behavior with fewer parts is non-infringing, so the key to writing great claims is to claim only the minimum number of moving parts, their relationship, and the behavior that those parts imbue in the invention. Further to the art of claiming, no claim will be allowed if it does not have proper antecedent basis in the specification, i.e. It is drawn and described in functional detail sufficient to determine that if made it will work. Further, no claim will be allowed if it does not have a definite presentation in which the language that is used in each stage of the claim is properly introduced and used consistently throughout and relate directly to the stated "where in" and "such that" offerings of the claim

GLOSSARY - Key terms used that are integral to the Schwartz Method

This GLOSSARY is ordered to facilitate an understanding of the language and guidance I used in creating the IP SAVYS book and the IP-BC course. To make this GLOSSARY a practical resource, I have ordered the terms in a sequence based on their relationship, one to the other, rather than in an alphabetic order. Review the terms in this order and develop a functional knowledge of their use and how they interoperate to deliver the TSM promise of forming airtight utility patents.

UPL and GP
Universal patenting language (UPL) and guiding principles (GP)

IP SAVVY cohorts use the universal patenting language to express their inventive matter in a form that is suitable for patent preparation. The vocabulary for UPL is found in the Claim Template. Each of the clauses and terms in that form represent the critical elements you must describe in relationship to your preferred embodiment in order to complete a patent application. The guiding principles of

TSM take shape around the claim template and how the invention disclosure patent application workbook (IDPAW) is formed.

There are two key aspects to this. (1) the linked set of loops on how the order of creation flows from section A with a drawing, to section C with a layman's claim, to section D where you explain the detailed description for that iteration of the P-E you are working on.

The other dimension is the 85%-15% GP. The fundamental idea is that 85% of what you are going to do with the patent draft is pre-determined and readily formed if and only if you get the 15% of enablement right the first time.

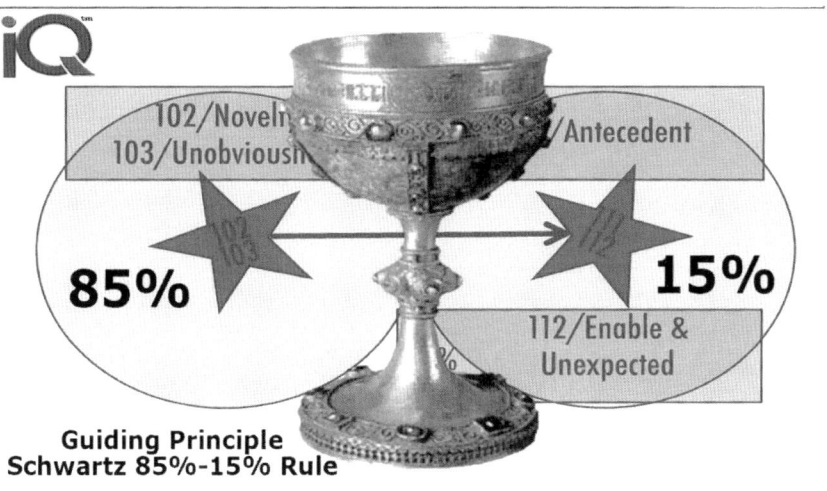

Fig. GP 85%-15% rule

So, the second aspect, (2), of the Schwartz 85%-15% rule stipulates that 15% of your interim patent draft is driven by your representation of enablement for the best mode of the invention, known to you at that time. The other 85% forms around that enablement in more or less the same way, independent of the field of invention you are in. The Schwartz patent rubric delivers on the paradigm that what you see is not how you get it by showing the way to iteratively create the core components of a utility patent application, without using an invention disclosure document to convey your inventive matter to anyone else.

IP-BC
Intellectual Property BoostCamp

This course is the complementary teaching to the IP SAVVYS book. It is comprised of four learning experiences:

IP-BC/ENTRY, IP-BC/INTERMEDIATE, IP-BC/ADVANCED, and IP-BC/ADVANCED-PRACTITIONER. Each level consists of modules. M#0 is comprised of Schwartz's opus webcast with a broad brush break down of the IP journey. M#1, the IP Corridor of Uncertainty, takes slow jams the journey in sections for each of the steps, exposing the potholes that lie ahead. M#2 is a detailed workflow of the Schwartz Method. M#3 is the 30-Day IP Challenge where you take your own IP and apply the Schwartz Method to develop a UCD.

P-E
Preferred-Embodiment

The P-E is the object of your patent application. It is the most current iteration of the invention that comprises the minimal number of elements (where each element has a name or label with a functional purpose), supports enablement (i.e., it works), and offers the unexpected benefit or outcome your invention seeks to deliver. The origin of the P-E can and should be traced to the flash of insight by the lead inventor, the moment the object of invention was conceived. The P-E will change until it stops changing. When it stops changing, you are ready to take the layman's claim description of it and turn that into a legally scoped claim as part of your filing package.

BBT
Big Bang Theory of IP Capitalization

BBT is the single unifying idea of IP SAVVYS and IP-BC. It offers a framework for integrating the preparation of iterative patent drafts with your product development lifecycle. The theory breaks down the steps that occur before and after T = 0 (notice of allowance/market entry). In the world of commercialization, people are very familiar with the steps that occur for business development, all related to the exploitation of an innovation. BBT seeks to visit the steps leading up to T = 0, walking backward in time to the conception of the inventive matter (flash of genius), and moving forward iteratively until the notice of allowance, when the universe is created in the Big Bang moment. BBT takes the point of view that the world turns on when an NOA is conferred by the US Patent Office on the owner who filed. Taking the inventor point of view from T = −5 (initial conception) to T = −1 (filing and first office action), BBT exposes the driving forces behind the patenting process, in each time interval before market entry. By doing so, BBT exposes the differing goals and objectives among all of the players in the IP hunt, from CEO to R&D/engineering and marketing/business development. It also offers a framework that can meld these conflicting points of view to build trust and efficiency in the development and delivery of utility compliant patent applications, prepared right the first time, and filed first.

IDPAW
Invention Disclosure Patent Application Workbook

The IDPAW is your patent application preparation workbook. It is comprised of entries using the UPL claim framework, formed in a loop using the "ABCDEF" GP sequence of creation with the

Schwartz Method (TSM) templates. The Schwartz Method provides an iterative way to develop an airtight, utility compliant patent draft during each step of the product development life cycle, by reverse engineering what a utility patent is and establishing the order of creation in what will become a utility compliant disclosure (UCD). The Schwartz Patent Rubric dynamically and dialectically manipulates the IDPAW and the claim template to inform the entry of each of the elements that will eventually be used to translate the idea to a patent. It's akin to making a jig-saw puzzle of a face. Start with the corners, find the nose and you're on your way to completion. By reverse engineering what a patent is from the section-by-section (1-6) MPEP document into a template sequenced by the order in which the patentable invention is created (ABCDEF), you only have to fill out the parts you know about at each step, starting with the corners (your classification and the terms from your P-E) and the nose (your layman's claim of the P-E). During each step, keep focused on filling in more and more of the required elements of the IDPAW, until you have completed the jigsaw puzzle and all of its features. The sequence of invention creation/disclosure/and claiming is iterative and dialectical. Once a complete version of the IDPAW/Claim template is rendered for a P-E of your intention, it can be converted into the target UCD, and then formatted, section by section using the MPEP utility patent application structure. The UCD is the intermediate form that will become your UCPA.

TSM
The Schwartz Method

The Schwartz Method is the proven, foolproof sequence of steps you take using the IDPAW and Claim template, enabling you to convert your idea from conception to a UCD and finally into a

UCPA. The iterative sequence is broken down into four intervals, and depending on how much you know about your invention, TSM guides you through the completion of the templates until you have your finally vetted version for your P-E. When the iterations stop, you're ready to convert your finally edited layman's claim into a legally scoped claim in a drafted utility compliant patent filing as part of your submission DOC PAK. The Schwartz Method ensures that you are de-risking your pre-patent document from rule 101, 102, 103, 111, 112, and 113 rejections, any, or all of which can occur in your first office action during the prosecution phase. The Schwartz Method utilizes the 85 percent/15 percent rule, one of the master guiding principles, to allow TSM to be used for utility patent drafting in any classification area. See the complete IP-BC course and especially level IP-BC/ADVANCED to find out more about this rule and guiding principle.

UCD
Utility Compliant Disclosure

A UCD is the output or completion of one version of a complete IDPAW/Claim template iteration, including at least one layman's claim of the P-E. It is progressively de-risked by ensuring that there is antecedent reference, no ambiguity, and that a complete description of enablement is made that would allow another skilled in the art of your classification to practice your invention. This is one of the key requirements for getting a patent application finally approved.

UCPA
Utility Compliant Patent Application

A UCPA is the edited version of a UCD that has been proofed and reviewed by a competent patent drafting person, whether an internal member of your IP counsel, or an outside IP patent counsel. It is fileable as either a provisional patent application (with at least one claim) or as a full non-provisional patent application. In the UCPA, you form an MPEP compliant patent application as a legal document incorporating a properly scoped legalese version of your claim. When and only when you're satisfied with your representation of enablement do you develop the final versions of the other sections of the MPEP compliant filing document. If you use the TSM model, then your patenting step is completed as a translation by cutting, pasting, and editing the set of finally approved claims, ensuring that the prepared paper is de-risked from FOARs before filing. This document will include all of the "boiler plate" text elements for a section by section pre-patent draft that follows the MPEP section sequence.

DISCOUNT COUPON CODE for IP-BC/ADVANCED

The IP-BC course, for everything related to utility patents, is the only on-line patenting course you will ever need to take. It provides an entire do it almost all yourself, DIAAY, framework for securing an airtight utility patent filed right the first time and de-risked for fatal office action rejections (FOARs).

To get your 25 percent discount on a single user copy of IP-BC/ADVANCED
  (1)   Go to the website: https://www.ipboostcamp.com.
  (2)   Put in the code: **ADV60DAY25OFF**

May the Schwartz be with you...